The International Business Environment

A Handbook for Managers and Executives

Warnock Davies

CRC Press
Taylor & Francis Group
Boca Raton   London   New York

CRC Press is an imprint of the
Taylor & Francis Group, an **informa** business
A PRODUCTIVITY PRESS BOOK

Contents

Preface

There are many factors that differentiate the conduct of international business (IB) from the conduct of domestic business. These include governmental, intergovernmental, systemic, and cultural factors that regulate, facilitate, and/or complicate the operations of companies engaged in the conduct of international business. These factors can be referred to collectively as the IB environment.

The elements of the IB environment include tariff and non-tariff barriers, antidumping duties, subsidies and countervailing duties, entry and post-entry barriers to foreign direct investment, political risk, the General Agreement on Tariffs and Trade and other global instruments, the World Trade Organization and other global mechanisms, regional trade blocs (which include free trade areas and customs unions), bilateral trade and investment agreements, the conflict of laws, dispute settlement mechanisms, and systemic and cultural differences.

The purpose of this book is to provide managers and executives with concise and incisive information on each of the elements of the IB environment—and on related terms, concepts, principles, and practices.

Design, uses, and format

The book has been designed for use as a handbook and reference book by managers and executives—and for use as a text in corporate seminars, executive development programs, and MBA programs.

Because the IB environment is a socio-political-economic construct the book's discussion of the elements employs both business and non-business disciplines. The non-business disciplines include international relations, international law, and (in the last chapter) sociology and cultural anthropology. The book relies primarily on original source materials, which are listed in section B1 of the bibliography, and makes extensive use of examples.

To facilitate its use as a handbook and reference book, the format uses three levels of headings and subheadings, short paragraphs, and vertical lists; the examples are separated from the body of the text; the bibliography listings include URLs; and chapter endnotes are used to cross-reference key terms, concepts, principles, sources, and subject areas. Also, headings and subheadings have been numbered to facilitate cross-referencing.

The US edition

The concepts and principles discussed in the book are global, but the examples are edition-specific. More than half of the examples in this United States (US) edition refer to trade to or from the US; foreign direct investment in or from the US; global, regional, or bilateral instruments or mechanisms that include US participation; US participation in international commercial disputes; or other situations that involve the US government or a US corporation.

Warnock Davies

Section I

Introduction

1 The elements

Contents

1.1 Business environments

The factors that influence the survival, success, and sustainability of a company's operations[1] can be classified as either internal or external.[2] A business environment is a socio-political-economic construct—and the sum of the external factors that govern or influence the conduct of business within a particular geographical area.

1.1.1 Domestic business environments

The term *domestic business* refers to commercial activities that occur within the borders of a nation-state.[3] A domestic business environment is the sum of the external factors that govern or influence the conduct of business within a nation-state.

The elements of domestic business environments include governmental policies, laws, regulations, rules, requirements, taxes, fees, mandated expenses, decisions, and actions; infrastructure and utilities; legal, financial, political, economic, and social systems; material, financial, and human resources; and operating conditions that are influenced by customers and/or competitors.

1.1.2 International business environments

The term *international business* refers to commercial activities that cross the borders of a nation-state.[4]

The international business environment is the sum of the governmental, intergovernmental, and systemic factors that (1) govern or influence the conduct of international business, and (2) are not present in domestic business environments.

1.2 The elements of the IB environment

The elements of the IB environment can be grouped into three primary categories: (1) regulatory elements, (2) facilitating elements, and (3) complicating elements. The sub-categories in each of these groups are shown in Figure 1.1.

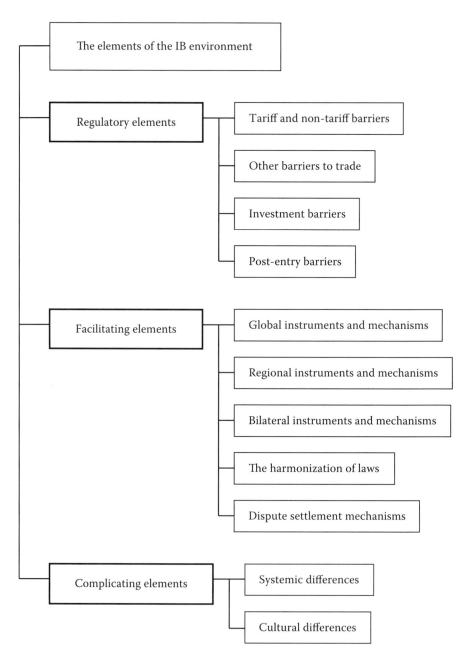

Figure 1.1   The elements of the IB environment.

The classification of regulatory, facilitating, and complicating elements is based on their operational significance. The term *operational significance* refers to how, and to what degree, an element affects the operations of companies engaged in the conduct of international business.

1.2.1 Regulatory elements

The *regulatory elements* of the IB environment are the policies, laws, regulations, rules, requirements, decisions, and actions that are implemented by governments of single nation-states—and that restrict or regulate international trade[5] and/or foreign direct investment.[6]

These elements can be grouped into four sub-categories:

- Tariff and non-tariff barriers
- Other barriers to trade
- Investment barriers
- Post-entry barriers

Regulatory elements are the most dominant elements of the IB environment because: (1) they restrict or regulate the conduct of IB; (2) they apply directly to the operations of companies engaged in the conduct of IB; and (3) they carry the force of national governmental authority.

The authority of a national government to restrict or regulate the conduct of commerce that crosses the borders of its nation-state is contained in the concept of sovereignty.[7]

The regulatory elements are discussed in Chapters 2 to 5.

1.2.2 Facilitating elements

The *facilitating elements* of the IB environment are the written agreements and the organizational and functional entities that are created and controlled by the governments of two or more nation-states—and are referred to as *intergovernmental instruments and mechanisms.*[8]

These elements can be grouped into five sub-categories:

- Global instruments and mechanisms
- Regional instruments and mechanisms
- Bilateral instruments and mechanisms
- Instruments and mechanisms for the harmonization of laws
- Dispute settlement mechanisms

Intergovernmental instruments and mechanisms: (1) provide the framework and the systems that facilitate the operation of the IB environment, (2) facilitate the reduction of trade and investment barriers, (3) facilitate the harmonization of laws and the settlement of disputes, and (4) govern or influence how national governments treat companies engaged in the conduct of IB.

The dominant facilitating instruments in the IB environment are the General Agreement on Tariffs and Trade (GATT) and other World Trade Organization (WTO) instruments. The dominant facilitating mechanism is the WTO.[9]

The facilitating elements are discussed in Chapters 6 to 9.

1.2.3 Complicating elements

The *complicating elements* of the IB environment are the differences in legal, financial, political, economic, and social systems in different countries,[10] which include differences in currencies, laws, languages and cultures.

These elements can be grouped into two sub-categories:

* Systemic differences
* Cultural differences[11]

The IB environment does not include the elements of domestic business environments. But differences in the systemic and cultural elements of business environments in different countries create discrete elements that influence the conduct of international business—and are elements of the IB environment.

Systemic and cultural differences neither regulate nor facilitate the conduct of international business. These differences can, however, make the conduct of IB more complex and difficult than the conduct of domestic business.

The complicating elements are discussed in Chapter 10.

Endnotes

1. The term *operations* refers to a company's revenue-producing activities.
2. The terms internal and external refer more to control than to where a function is located or occurs. Internal factors include resources, conditions, decisions, and actions that are managed or controlled by a company's managers and executives—even if these factors (such as supply-chain management, marketing, and corporate social responsibility operations) are located or occur outside the company. External factors include resources, conditions, decisions, and actions that govern or influence a company's operations—that are not managed or controlled by a company's managers and executives.
3. The terms *nation-state*, *state*, and *country* are discussed in Chapter 6, Section 6.1.
4. In the conduct of international commercial relations, references to states or nation-states include separate customs territories. The term *separate customs territory* is discussed in Chapter 6, Section 6.1.1.3.
5. The term *international trade* is discussed in Chapter 2, Section 2.1.
6. The term *foreign direct investment* is discussed in Chapter 4, Section 4.1.
7. The concept of sovereignty is discussed in Chapter 6, Section 6.1.2.
8. The terms *intergovernmental*, *instruments*, and *mechanisms* are discussed in Chapter 6, Sections 6.2, 6.3, and 6.4.
9. The GATT, other WTO instruments, and the WTO are discussed in Chapter 7.
10. The term *country* is discussed in Chapter 6, Section 6.1.1.2.
11. As discussed in Chapter 10, Section 10.2, cultural differences are a subcategory of social-system differences and are, therefore, systemic differences. It is customary practice, however, to treat cultural differences as a separate category.

Section II

Regulatory elements

2 Tariff and non-tariff barriers

Contents

2.1 The trade–investment dichotomy

All international commercial activity, which is referred to collectively as international business, can be classified as either *international trade* or *foreign investment*. These parts of IB are often referred to simply as trade and investment.[1]

In the conduct of IB, the term *international trade* refers to the cross-border sale and delivery—or purchase and delivery—of a product or service. The term *foreign investment* is discussed in Chapter 4, Section 4.1.

2.1.1 Barriers to IB

Elements of the IB environment that restrict or regulate the conduct of international business are referred to as *barriers*. Barriers to IB can be classified as either *trade barriers* or *investment barriers*.

Trade barriers, which are also called *barriers to trade*, are discussed in this chapter, in Chapter 3, and in some parts of Chapter 5. Investment barriers are discussed in Chapters 4 and 5.

2.1.2 Barriers to trade

A trade barrier is any action by the government of a nation-state that restricts or regulates trade.[2] Trade barriers can be divided into three categories: (1) tariff barriers, (2) non-tariff barriers, and (3) other barriers to trade.

2.2 Tariff barriers

A tariff, trade tariff, or customs tariff (1) is a set customs duty, (2) is on a published list, and (3) is applied to a category of products[3] entering or leaving a nation-state. Tariffs can be applied to exports, but in practice almost all tariffs are on imports.[4]

2.2.1 Tariff-related terms and definitions

2.2.1.1 Customs duties

Duties are a form of tax. The meaning of the term *tax* is extremely broad: It can refer to any compulsory payment that is levied on individuals, on companies, or on the sale or movement of products, and is payable to a government.

A duty is a tax that is levied on the sale or movement of a product. Duties that are applied to the sale or movement of a product within a nation-state are referred to as *excise duties*.[5]

The term *customs* refers to the government department that administers and collects duties levied on products entering or leaving a nation-state. Duties that are applied to products entering or leaving a nation-state are referred to broadly as *customs duties*.[6]

Customs duties include tariffs, safeguards, anti-dumping duties, and countervailing duties.[7]

2.2.1.2 Customs tariffs

The word *tariff* literally means a list of fixed prices or fees that is made public.[8] In international trade, the term *tariff* or *customs tariff* refers to a customs duty that is fixed, is listed on a customs tariff schedule, and applies to a particular HS product category[9] and to a product's country of origin.[10]

Customs tariffs are classified as either *ad valorem* tariffs or *specific duty* tariffs.[11]

2.2.1.3 Ad valorem tariffs

Most trade tariffs are *ad valorem*.[12] An *ad valorem* tariff is based on a product's monetary value, is referred to as a *tariff rate*, and is expressed as a percentage.

The US: Cars

The trade tariff on cars is usually an *ad valorem* tariff. For example, the tariff rate on cars entering the United States is 2.5 percent. Based on this tariff rate, if the value of a car entering the United States is $30,000, the tariff will be $750.

2.2.1.4 Specific duty tariffs

A *specific duty* tariff is an amount levied on each unit that is imported, or on each unit of quantity or weight that is imported. Specific duty tariffs are not expressed as a percentage, but as a monetary amount.

Indonesia: Rice

In 2011, the government of Indonesia applied a tariff of 450 rupiahs per kg on the importation of rice. This was a specific duty tariff, because it applied to the quantity (by weight) of the rice being imported. Based on this tariff, if the amount of rice being imported is 1,000 kg, the tariff will be 450,000 rupiahs.

2.2.1.5 Tariff rates and amounts

The *ad valorem* tariff rate, or specific duty tariff, is governed by a product's category and country of origin. The tariff rate or amount of tariff on a product is not affected by the identity of the company that produced or exported the product.

The term *tariff rate* or *rate* is sometimes used as a general term when referring to either a tariff rate or a specific duty. For example, the GATT uses the term *preferential rate* when referring to a preferential tariff rate or a preferential special duty.[13]

2.2.2 Product categories

The method for denominating tariff product categories, which is used by 177 nation-states and separate customs territories to classify products that account for 98 percent of international trade, is called the Harmonized System (HS).

2.2.2.1 HS codes

HS codes (which are also referred to as HS classification codes, customs tariff codes, tariff codes, and tariff headings) are part of the nomenclature and coding system contained in the International Convention on the Harmonized Commodity Description and Coding System (HS Convention).[14]

The HS uses more than 1,200 headings, which are grouped into 97 chapters and 21 sections. In the following examples, the first two digits are the chapter number, the first four digits are the heading number, and all six digits are the HS code.

HS codes for categories of cars and rice

870323   Motor cars and other motor vehicles principally designed for the transport of persons (other than those of heading 87.02), including station wagons and racing cars. Other vehicles, with spark-ignition internal combustion reciprocating piston engine...Of a cylinder capacity exceeding 1,500 cc but not exceeding 3,000 cc
870324   Motor cars...Of a cylinder capacity exceeding 3,000 cc
100610   Rice in the husk (paddy or rough)
100620   Husked (brown) rice

2.2.2.2 The extension of HS codes

Article 3 of the HS Convention says the six-digit numerical HS codes must not be modified, but a national government may modify the text to comply with domestic law.

Nation-states may use an additional one or two pairs of digits to make product categories more specific, which results in eight- or ten-digit codes.

The US: HTSUS

The Harmonized Tariff Schedule of the United States (HTSUS) came into effect in 1989.[15] HTSUS uses the HS codes and coding system; includes 1,700 headings, 99 chapters, and 22 sections; and uses ten-digit codes.

In some cases, the last pair of digits in a ten-digit code is used to facilitate the compilation of trade statistics.

2.2.3 Country of origin

In international trade, the term *country of origin* does not refer to the nation-state from where a product was exported, but refers to the nation-state where the product was grown, produced, or manufactured.

A product's country of origin affects its tariff rate and origin marking requirements (labeling), and can also affect other trade-related factors including quotas,[16] safeguard measures,[17] anti-dumping duties,[18] countervailing duties,[19] and preferential tariffs[20]—and the implementation of governmental procurement programs, trade embargos, and the Generalized System of Preferences (GSP).[21]

Determining the country of origin of agricultural products (such as apples, rice, or cotton) is not difficult, because their country of origin is the country in which they are grown. It can, however, be difficult to determine the country of origin of manufactured products (such as shoes, clothes, or computers)—which can include materials, parts, and components from different countries, and can include research, design, development, and manufacturing processes that occur in two or more countries.

2.2.3.1 Rules of origin

The criteria used for determining a product's country of origin are referred to as *rules of origin* (ROO). ROO are divided into two categories: preferential and non-preferential.

Preferential rules of origin apply to trade that occurs between members of a free trade area (FTA).[22] Each FTA sets its own rules of origin. Preferential ROO are discussed in Chapter 8, Section 8.3.1.5.

Non-preferential ROO apply to trade that does not occur between member states of an FTA.

2.2.3.2 Non-preferential rules of origin

The governments of nation-states have created two global instruments[23] that contain non-preferential rules of origin: the International Convention on the Simplification and Harmonization of Customs Procedures, which is referred to as the Kyoto Convention,[24] and the Agreement on Rules of Origin.[25] These instruments provide general standards and specific criteria for determining country of origin.

2.2.3.3 Substantial transformation

When the manufacture of a product includes processes in more than one country, the Kyoto Convention says its "origin should be determined according to the substantial transformation criterion."[26] The Agreement on Rules of Origin says the term *substantial transformation* refers to "the country where the last substantial transformation has been carried out."[27]

There is, however, no generally agreed upon method for determining what constitutes a substantial transformation, and the international harmonization[28] of this aspect of ROO has proven to be one of the most intractable issues in international trade.[29]

Most countries use one of three methods for determining substantial transformation:

1. The change-in-tariff-classification method defines a substantial transformation as a process that results in a change in two or more of the digits in a product's HS code.[30]
2. The value-added or *ad valorem*–percentage method says substantial transformation is a process that adds substantially to the value of a product.[31]
3. The special-processing rule uses a list of special-processing operations that are seen as effecting a substantial transformation of a product.

In some cases, countries modify one of these methods, combine elements from different methods, or use their own method.

The US: Change in name, character, or use

In the US, rules of origin are administered by the US Customs and Border Protection (CBP) of the US Department of Homeland Security. In cases that require the application of non-preferential ROO (that is, ROO that apply to trade that does not occur between members of an FTA), the CBP uses the substantial transformation criterion on a case-by-case basis, "based on a change in name/character/use method (i.e., an article that consists in whole or in part of materials from more than one country is a product of the country in which it has been substantially transformed into a new and different article of commerce with a name, character, and use distinct from that of the article or articles from which is was so transformed)."[32]

In 2008, the CBP proposed changing its case-by-case non-preferential ROO by expanding the preferential ROO contained in the North American Free Trade Agreement (NAFTA),[33] which use the change-in-tariff-classification method. The CBP subsequently decided not to proceed with this proposal.

2.2.4 *The purposes of tariffs*

The governments of nation-states use tariffs: (1) to protect the production, manufacture, and sale of domestic products, and to protect domestic companies, industries, and jobs; (2) to address balance of payments problems; (3) to generate revenue; and/or (4) to limit exports.

2.2.4.1 *To protect domestic products, companies, industries, and jobs*

About 2,400 years ago, Socrates argued that the first role of government is to protect society. Most governmental leaders believe that every nation-state has the right and the duty to protect its economic viability—and to protect the economic welfare of its citizens.

Most governmental leaders also believe that to protect their nation-state's economic viability, and to protect the economic welfare of their citizens, they must protect their country's companies, industries, and jobs—by protecting the production, manufacture, and sale of domestic products.

When a government applies a tariff to an imported product, this adds to the cost of the product and increases the price at which the product must be sold to make a profit. By adding to the price at which imported products are sold, tariffs provide a competitive advantage to domestic producers and manufacturers.

When a tariff is used primarily to protect domestic products—and/or to protect domestic companies, industries, or jobs—it is referred to as a protective tariff.

Canada: Cheese

To protect the Canadian dairy and poultry industries, the government of Canada has established a *supply management* system that includes three pillars: production controls, price controls,[34] and import controls. The import controls include a 246 percent tariff on imported cheese.

The protection of domestic products, companies, industries, and/or jobs—and the need by some governments to manage their balance of payments—is why almost all tariffs are on imports.

2.2.4.2 *To address balance of payments problems*

Some nation-states have balance of payments problems, because the value of their imports far exceeds the value of their exports. To address these problems, some nation-states, and especially least-developed countries,[35] use tariffs to reduce the number or amount of non-essential imports.[36]

2.2.4.3 *To generate revenue*

For some nation-states, the primary reason for the use of tariffs has been to raise revenue.

The US: Revenue

The United States became a nation-state in 1789. Due to the cost of the war of independence between the American colonies and England,[37] the US began with a large national debt. Also, it had no source of revenue with which to pay this debt or to pay for the operating and administrative costs of the government.

To address this problem, the Congress of the United States passed the Hamilton Tariff of 1789, which levied tariffs on a list of imported products. In 1792, tariff revenues accounted for 100 percent of the US budget.

Tariffs continued to be the largest single source of revenue for the US government until 1913, when it established an income tax. By 1944, revenues from tariffs had declined to about one percent of the US budget—and since then have continued to average about one percent.

Ukraine: Revenue

In December 2014, in an attempt to reduce its budget deficit and satisfy foreign lender governments and the International Monetary Fund (IMF), the Supreme Council of Ukraine adopted measures that included additional tariffs on imports.

2.2.4.4 To limit exports

Most tariffs are on imports, but some tariffs are on exports. Some nation-states use export tariffs for the same purpose as the temporary export duties discussed in Sections 2.3.3.2 and 2.3.3.3.

2.2.4.5 Combinations

Decisions by national governments related to the use of tariffs can be influenced by two or more reasons.

The US: Revenue and protection

In 1789, when the US Secretary of the Treasury, Alexander Hamilton, recommended the use of tariffs to raise revenue, he also argued that the application of tariffs would discourage imports and protect domestic industries.

2.2.5 The decline in the role of tariff barriers

In the past, tariffs were the most widely used barriers to trade—and were the dominant regulatory element in the IB environment. Governments could protect their nation-states' products, companies, industries, and jobs by applying protective tariffs.

But the extraordinary success of the GATT,[38] the WTO, and regional trade blocs[39] at reducing tariffs has severely limited the ability of governments to use tariffs as a protective mechanism. This has resulted in an increase in the use and significance of non-tariff barriers.

2.3 Non-tariff barriers

A non-tariff barrier (NTB) is a trade barrier that is not a tariff. Like tariff barriers, NTBs can apply to both imports and exports, but most NTBs apply to imports.

NTBs can be divided into three groups: (1) technical barriers to trade, (2) non-technical barriers to trade, and (3) NTBs on exports.

2.3.1 Technical barriers to trade

Article XX of the GATT includes a list of *general exceptions* that allow WTO members to use measures that restrict trade. These NTBs are referred to as *technical barriers to trade*.[40]

The most widely used and significant technical barriers to trade are contained in Article XX.(b), which refers to measures that are "necessary to protect human, animal or plant life or health."

2.3.1.1 Human life and health

Measures that protect human life, health, or safety include restrictions and regulations such as labeling requirements on food; restrictions on the importation of agricultural products that contain pesticide or chemical residues, and on textiles and leather that have been treated with certain dyes; and safety certification requirements for electrical products.

The US: FDA and FSIS

The US Food and Drug Administration (FDA), which maintains inspection offices in the United States and nine other countries, is responsible for "ensuring that the nation's food supply for human and animal consumption is safe, sanitary, wholesome, and properly labeled."[41]

The FDA's responsibilities cover all imported food except meat, poultry, and processed eggs, which come under the Food Safety and Inspection Service (FSIS) of the US Department of Agriculture (USDA).

The FSIS is responsible for approving and auditing countries that may export meat, poultry, and processed eggs to the US, for determining that these countries have inspection programs that are equivalent to those in the US, and for administering the reinspection program in the US.[42]

2.3.1.2 Animal and plant life or health

Measures that protect animal or plant life or health include restrictions and regulations relating to the health and protection of animals, plants, and the physical environment—such as requirements related to the recycling, reuse, biodegradability, and disposal of packaging.

The US: APHIS

The USDA's Animal and Plant Health Inspection Service (APHIS) is responsible for "keeping US agricultural industries free from pests and diseases."[43]

2.3.1.3 Technical barriers and protection

Article XX of the GATT says that technical barriers to trade must not be used as "a means of arbitrary or unjustifiable discrimination between countries" or as "a disguised restriction on international trade."

But technical barriers to trade are frequently used by national governments to protect their country's products, companies, industries, and/or jobs.

Germany: Electrical tools

In 2005, German Customs seized a large quantity of Chinese-made electrical tools (including those made by German companies ALDI and Bosch), on the grounds that these products contained a chemical carcinogen called PAH. The German government also started inspecting all Chinese-made electrical tools, and instructed retailers to not sell these products.

These actions appear to have been an unjustifiable discrimination between countries and a disguised restriction on international trade, because, at the time, neither Germany nor the European Union (EU) had standards relating to PAH in electrical tools, and because these actions were applied solely to products made in China.

2.3.2 *Non-technical barriers to trade*

Non-technical barriers to trade include: (1) administrative rules and requirements, (2) quotas, (3) safeguards, and (4) systemic and structural factors.

2.3.2.1 *Administrative rules and requirements*

The purpose of trade-related administrative rules and requirements is to facilitate the implementation of a nation-state's trade policies, and to regulate its international trade.

Administrative rules and requirements NTBs include:

- Restrictions on payments for imports[44]
- Local content requirements[45]
- Market access[46] barriers (including structural barriers)
- Restrictions on imports related to production or manufacturing methods, such as restrictions on the importation of shrimp that were harvested using methods or equipment that threaten sea turtles, and restrictions on the importation of products that include child-labor content
- Documentation requirements and customs, inspection, and certification procedures
- Administrative, customs, inspection, and certification fees

NTBs associated with administrative rules and requirements include:

- Administrative delays, including customs delays, and delays in anti-dumping and subsidy investigations[47]
- Lack of transparency in regulations[48]
- Inadequate protection for intellectual property rights
- The absence of established procedures[49]
- The inconsistent application of laws, rules, and regulations

The US: Country of origin rulings

In the US, delays in country-of-origin rulings by the CBP Office of Regulations and Rulings[50] can act as NTBs, because 65 percent of these rulings take up to three months to complete, and 35 percent take more than three months.[51]

In practice, administrative rules and requirements associated with technical barriers to trade can have indirect or secondary affects that act as non-technical barriers to trade.

China: CCC

The Compulsory Product Certification System, which is administered by the Certification and Accreditation Administration of China (CNCA), requires that all electrical products (and many other products) sold in China must carry the China Compulsory Certification Mark (CCC). The CCC requirement applies to products made in China and to imported products.

In addition to testing products for safety and quality, the CNCA applies quality process standards to the factories where products are manufactured. Factories in foreign countries that make products for export to China must be inspected and certified for compliance with CCC standards.

The purpose of the CCC requirement is to ensure the safety and quality of electrical and other products, and is, therefore, a technical barrier to trade.52 But because the costs and time delays associated with CCC inspection requirements for foreign manufacturers frequently result in expensive and complex inspection and certification procedures, these requirements can also act as a non-technical barrier to trade.

Some administrative rules and requirements NTBs are the same as, or similar to, some of the post-entry barriers discussed in Chapter 5.

2.3.2.2 *Quotas*

A quota is a quantitative restriction on the number or amount of a product category that may be imported or exported during a specific period.[53] Quotas allow nation-states to regulate the volume of, or tariff rate on, imports or exports of a specific product category from or to a specific country.

There are two types of quotas: absolute quotas, and tariff rate quotas.

1. *Absolute quotas*: An absolute quota sets the maximum number or amount of a product category that may be imported from or exported to a nation-state during a specific period.

The US and Japan: Cars

A series of agreements that were entered into by the governments of the United States and Japan between 1981 and 1994 applied quotas that restricted the number of Japanese cars that could be imported into the US each year.

China and the EU: Textiles

From 2005 to 2007, the government of China applied quantitative limits that restricted the amount of ten categories of textiles that could be exported to the European Union.

2. *Tariff rate quotas.* A tariff-rate quota (TRQ) sets the maximum number or amount of a product category that may be imported from a nation-state at a preferential in-quota tariff (which can be as low as zero tariff) during a specific period. When the number or amount allowed by the quota has been reached, additional imports can continue at the non-preferential over-quota tariff.

Canada and the EU: Cheese

In 2013, Canada and the EU entered into a Comprehensive Economic and Trade Agreement (CETA), which eliminated 98 percent of tariffs on Canadian products entering the EU, and gave products from the EU greater access to Canada.

One of the provisions of the CETA is that 29,000 million tonnes of cheese[54] from the EU may enter Canada annually at a zero in-quota tariff (that is, duty free), after which EU cheese imports will be subject to an over-quota tariff of 246 percent.

The US and sub-Saharan Africa: AGOA

Under the Africa Growth and Opportunity Act (AGOA) of 2000, the United States maintains duty-free TRQs on a wide range of products, which include dairy, beef, cotton, peanuts, peanut butter and paste, tobacco, sugar and sugar-containing products, textiles, and wearing apparel,[55] from about 40 eligible countries in sub-Saharan Africa.

Since 1995, most quotas have been tariff-rate quotas. The Agreement on Agriculture, which is one of the 60 agreements concluded in 1994 during the Uruguay Round of GATT negotiations,[56] prohibits the use of absolute quotas on agriculture trade between WTO member states. The *tariffication* provisions of the agreement, however, allow the use of tariff-rate quotas.

2.3.2.3 Safeguards

The term *safeguards* refers to functional mechanisms[57] for limiting imports that may be used by specific categories of nation-states, or by a nation-state that needs to take an *emergency action*.

Article XII of the GATT, Safeguard the Balance of Payments, allows least-developed countries that have balance of payment problems to use quotas to limit imports.[58]

Article XVIII of the GATT, Governmental Assistance to Economic Development, allows developing countries that are "in the early stages of development" to restrict the quantity or value of imports.

Article XIX of the GATT, Emergency Action on Imports of Particular Products, and the WTO Safeguards Agreement allow WTO members to limit temporarily the importation of a product category if an increase in imports could cause serious injury to a domestic industry.

2.3.2.4 Systemic and structural factors

In some cases, a systemic or structural element of an importing county's domestic business environment can act as a non-tariff barrier to trade.

Some of these systemic or structural elements are governmental (such as the NTBs associated with administrative rules and requirements, which are discussed in Section 2.3.2.1), but some are non-governmental. For example, some of the non-governmental systemic differences discussed in Chapter 10, Section 10.1, can have the effect of restricting trade; and some of the non-governmental industry-specific structural elements in an importing country can be seen as acting as barriers to trade.

The US and Japan: Cars

In the 1980s, US car manufacturers argued that the principal reason they were unable to penetrate the Japanese car market was that, in Japan, the networks of new car distributors and dealers were owned and/or controlled by Japanese car manufacturers, and that this was a structural barrier to trade.

2.3.3 NTBs on exports

Like tariffs, most NTBs apply to imports, but some NTBs apply to exports. NTBs that limit exports include the following:

2.3.3.1 Restrictions on exports on the grounds of national security

The US: DDTC and USML

The US Government views the sale, export, and re-transfer of defense articles and defense services as an integral part of safeguarding US national security and furthering US foreign policy objectives. The Directorate of Defense Trade Controls (DDTC)...is charged with controlling the export and temporary import of defense articles and defense services covered by the United States Munitions List (USML).[59]

As of 2014, there were 26 countries covered by the DDTC's Country Policies and Embargos.[60]

2.3.3.2   *Restrictions contained in voluntary export restraint and orderly marketing agreements*

The purpose of *voluntary export restraint agreements* and *orderly marketing agreements* between governments is to prevent a surge in exports that could injure an industry in an importing country. Exporting countries use these agreements to dissuade an importing country from applying trade barriers to their products.[61]

The US and Japan: Cars

The agreements between the United States and Japan, discussed in Section 2.3.2.2, which restricted the number of Japanese cars that could be imported annually into the United States, were voluntary export restraint agreements.

In the 1981 agreement, the government of Japan agreed to limit the annual exportation of cars to the United States to 1.68 million. This limit was increased in subsequent agreements, and the agreements ended in 1994.

China and the EU: Textiles

As discussed in Section 2.3.2.2, in 2005, the government of China applied export duties to Chinese-made textiles being exported to the EU. China subsequently entered into an "orderly marketing agreement" with the EU, which included temporary duties and quotas.

If these duties (and the duties in the next example) had been permanent, they would have been tariffs. Because these duties were temporary, they were NTBs.

Since 1995, the Uruguay Round agreements[62] have severely limited the use of voluntary export restraint agreements by WTO member states.

2.3.3.3   *Export duties to conserve national resources and limit the export of energy-intensive products.*

China: Aluminum, nickel, and copper

From 2005 to 2009, China applied duties on the export of aluminum, nickel, and copper—to conserve these national resources for use in China, and to discourage the use of China as the location for the processing of energy-intensive materials and products.

2.3.4 Other barriers to trade

The anti-dumping duties, subsidies, countervailing duties, and the politicization of trade barriers discussed in Chapter 3 act as barriers to trade.

It could be argued that because these elements are barriers to trade and are not tariffs, they are, by definition, non-tariff barriers.[63] In practice, however, the term *non-tariff barrier* is not used when referring to the elements discussed in Chapter 3.

Endnotes

1. Davies, "Global Business Strategy," 83.
2. In some cases, non-governmental factors act as barriers that restrict trade. This is discussed in Section 2.3.2.4.
3. In this book, the term *product* or *products* covers both products and services.
4. The reason most tariffs are on imports is discussed in Section 2.2.4.1.
5. Excise duties are sometimes referred to as *inland taxes.*
6. Customs duties are sometimes referred to as *border taxes.*
7. Safeguards are discussed in Section 2.3.2.3; anti-dumping duties are discussed in Chapter 3, Section 3.1; countervailing duties are discussed in Chapter 3, Section 3.2.
8. The word *tariff* comes from the Italian *tariffa*: list of prices or book of rates, which is derived from the Arabic *ta'rif*: to notify or announce.
9. HS product categories are discussed in Section 2.2.2.
10. A product's country of origin is discussed in Section 2.2.3.
11. Nation-states sometimes use a combination of an *ad valorem* tariff and a specific duty tariff, which is called a *compound tariff.*
12. The term *ad valorem* is Latin for "according to value."
13. GATT, Articles I, 4; II, 1, c; and V, 6. Preferential tariffs are discussed in Chapter 8, Sections 8.3.1.1 and 8.3.1.7.
14. Conventions are discussed in Chapter 6, Section 6.3.2. The HS Convention was adopted by the contracting parties of the Customs Co-operation Council (CCC) in 1983, and entered into force in 1988. In 1994 the CCC changed its name to the World Customs Organization (WCO).
15. The HTSUS replaced the Tariff Schedules of the United States (TSUS).
16. Quotas are discussed in Section 2.3.2.2.
17. Safeguards are discussed in Section 2.3.2.3.
18. Anti-dumping duties are discussed in Chapter 3, Section 3.1.
19. Countervailing duties are discussed in Chapter 3, Section 3.2.
20. See Endnote 13.
21. The GSP provides preferential tariffs on products from developing countries and territories.
22. FTAs are discussed in Chapter 8, Section 8.3.
23. Intergovernmental instruments are discussed in Chapter 6, Section 6.3.
24. The Kyoto Convention was created by the Customs Co-operation Council (now the WCO), entered into force in 1974, and has been periodically revised. The Kyoto Convention is distinct from the Kyoto Protocol (the United Nations Framework Convention on Climate Change).
25. The Agreement on Rules of Origin was created during the Uruguay Round of multilateral trade negotiations (which is discussed in Chapter 7, Section 7.3.2.2), and entered into force in 1995. It is administered jointly by the WTO and the WCO.
26. The Kyoto Convention, Specific Annex K, Chapter 1, rules of origin, 2 and 3.
27. The Agreement on Rules of Origin, Article 3(b).
28. The harmonization of laws is discussed in Chapter 9, Section 9.1.
29. The Harmonization Work Program (which was established by the Agreement on Rules of Origin), the WTO Committee on Rules of Origin (CRO) (which comes under the WTO Council for Trade in Goods), and the Technical Committee on Rules of Origin (which is a committee of the World Customs Organization) have been working on the

international harmonization of ROO since 1995. Most of this work has been on the cod-ification of substantial transformation methods. In 2010, the WTO CRO reported it had reached consensus on ROO for 1,528 of 2,739 product categories.

30. The change-in-tariff classification method, which is also called the tariff-shift method, is discussed in Chapter 8, Section 8.3.1.6, NAFTA. HS codes are discussed in Section 2.2.2.1.
31. The value-added method is discussed in Chapter 8, Section 8.3.1.6, the ASEAN FTA.
32. US Customs and Border Protection, *U.S. Rules of Origin*.
33. NAFTA ROO are discussed in Chapter 8, Section 8.3.1.6.
34. The Canadian supply management system controls the prices of milk, cheese, chicken, and eggs.
35. The term *least developed countries* refers to 48 countries on the United Nations LDC list.
36. For members of the WTO, this use of tariffs is governed by Article 9 of the 1994 *Understanding on the Balance-of-Payments Provisions of the General Agreement on Tariffs and Trade*.
37. The American War of Independence, also called the American Revolutionary War, 1775 to 1783.
38. The extraordinary success of the GATT at reducing tariffs is discussed in Chapter 7, Section 7.3.1.2.
39. Regional trade blocs are discussed in Chapter 8, Section 8.2.
40. The rules relating to the use of these NTBs are contained in the WTO Agreement on Technical Barriers to Trade.
41. USFDA, FDA 2013 Annual Report.
42. USDA, FSIS Office of International Affairs.
43. USDA, Animal and Plant Health.
44. Restrictions on foreign payments are discussed in Chapter 5, Section 5.2.1.
45. Local content requirements are discussed in Chapter 5, Sections 5.2.2 and 5.3.1.
46. In the conduct of international commerce, the term *market access* is defined by the WTO as "the conditions, tariff and non-tariff measures, agreed by members for the entry of specific goods into their markets." WTO Secretariat, Market access for goods.
47. Anti-dumping and subsidy investigations are discussed in Chapter 3, Sections 3.1.2 and 3.2.4.2.
48. Transparency is discussed in Chapter 5, Section 5.4.2.
49. The absence of established procedures is discussed in Chapter 5, Section 5.4.3.
50. The administration of ROO in the US is discussed in Section 2.2.3.3.
51. US Government Accountability Office, *U.S. Customs Service*.
52. Technical barriers to trade are discussed in Section 2.3.1.
53. Article XI of the GATT provides for the "General Elimination of Quantitative Restrictions," but includes a list of exceptions.
54. This tonnage is just under seven percent of Canada's annual domestic cheese market, which is about 420,000 tonnes.
55. The AGOA TRQs on clothing and some textiles are subject to the AGOA rules of ori-gin. Rules of origin are discussed in Section 2.2.3.1, and in Chapter 8, Sections 8.3.1.4 and 8.3.1.5.
56. The Uruguay Round of GATT negotiations is discussed in Chapter 7, Section 7.3.2.2.
57. Functional mechanisms are discussed in Chapter 6, Section 6.4.2.
58. The term *least developed countries* is discussed in Endnote 35.
59. US State Department, DDTC, Mission.

60. US State Department, DDTC, Policies and Embargos.
61. The terms *exporting county* and *importing country* are discussed in Chapter 6, Section 6.1.1.2.
62. The Uruguay Round agreements are discussed in Chapter 7, Section 7.3.2.2,
63. The term *non-tariff barrier* is defined at the beginning of Section 2.3.

3   Other barriers to trade

Contents

3.1 Anti-dumping duties

Article VI of the GATT defines dumping as when "products of one country are introduced into the commerce of another country at less than the normal value of the products."

The concept of dumping is unique to international commerce. When engaged in the conduct of domestic commerce in a free market economy, a company may sell its products at whatever price it chooses. In the conduct of international commerce, however, the GATT rules allow WTO members to apply anti-dumping duties as a trade remedy to offset or prevent dumping and to protect a domestic industry from injury.

3.1.1 The two-part test

Article VI of the GATT requires governments to use a two-part test when conducting anti-dumping investigations.

3.1.1.1 Part 1: Less than normal value

The government of the importing country must determine if the product was imported "at less than its normal value."[1] There are three methods for determining normal value:

1. Domestic price. In most cases, the term *normal value* refers to the price at which a product is sold in the domestic market of the exporting country, or in the domestic market of a surrogate third country.[2]

   If there is no "domestic price," because the product is not sold in the exporting country, normal value can be determined by using one of the following methods:
2. "The highest comparable price" at which the product is exported to a third country.
3. "The cost of production of the product in the country of origin[3] plus a reasonable addition for selling cost and profit."[4]

3.1.1.2 Part 2: Injury to a domestic industry

The government of the importing country must determine if the imported product has caused or threatens to cause "material injury to an established industry…or materially retards the establishment of a domestic industry"[5] in the importing country.

3.1.2 The two necessary conditions

Both conditions of the two-part test must be present for the government of the importing country to proceed with an anti-dumping investigation or to apply anti-dumping duties.

The US and nine other countries: Pipes and tubes used in the oil industry

In 2013, the US International Trade Commission (USITC) said it was pursuing an anti-dumping investigation because it had "determined that there is a reasonable indication that a US industry is materially injured by reason of imports of certain oil country tubular goods from India, [South] Korea, the Philippines, Saudi Arabia, Taiwan, Thailand, Turkey, Ukraine, and Vietnam that are allegedly sold in the United States at less than fair value"[6]

Australia and Greece: Currants

In 2014, the government of Australia announced that an earlier investigation had found Greek currants had been imported into Australia at "dumped prices"; that "the latest investigation has found dumping is still continuing"; that "the dumping of Greek currants into the Australian market resulted in injury to Australian manufacturers"—and that the government was applying anti-dumping duties of up to 8.1 percent on imported currants from Greece.[7]

If an anti-dumping investigation finds only one of the two necessary conditions is present, the importing country may not apply anti-dumping duties to the imported product.

The US, China, Germany, and Turkey: Wire rods

In 2005, the USITC investigated the importation of carbon and alloy steel wire rods from China, Germany, and Turkey. During the investigation, the steel manufacturers from these countries argued that: (1) imports of these products from China, Germany, and Turkey had declined in the first nine months of 2005, (2) demand for these products in the US exceeded supply, and (3) the profits of US wire rod makers had declined slightly in 2005, but were still higher than the average for previous years.

The USITC found that the products covered in this investigation had been imported at less than normal value—but also found the importation of these products had not caused or threatened to cause material injury to US manufacturers. Because only one of the two necessary conditions was present, the US government did not apply anti-dumping duties to these products.

3.1.3 Anti-dumping duties

The term *anti-dumping duties* (ADDs) refers to customs duties that are intended to offset the effects of a product being imported at less than normal value.

Anti-dumping duties are not tariffs: They are not set duties on a published list that are applied to a category of products. An ADD is a specific duty, which is applied to a specific product, which is imported from a specific country, by a specific company, at a specific price.

3.1.3.1 The purpose and level of anti-dumping duties

Anti-dumping duties are not intended to be punitive. Their purpose is to offset the less than normal value at which a product was imported—and to achieve parity between a product's normal value and the price at which it was imported—by adding to the price at which the product is sold in the importing country.

Because the purpose of an ADD is to achieve parity between a product's normal value and the price at which it was imported, the amount of an ADD applied by the government of an importing country may not exceed the margin of dumping. The term *margin of dumping* refers to the difference between the product's normal value and price at which the product was imported.

The EU, Argentina, and Indonesia: Biodiesel

In 2013, the EU imposed anti-dumping duties on imports of biodiesel[8] from Argentina and Indonesia. The European Commission said that "the bio-diesel anti-dumping duties do not constitute a punishment, but are imposed strictly to prevent further injury to the EU industry." The duties will be imposed "at the level of the injury margin," which for Argentina is between 22 and 25.7 percent, and for Indonesia is between 8.8 and 20.5 percent.[9]

3.1.3.2 Ad valorem and specific anti-dumping duties

An anti-dumping duty can be either an *ad valorem* duty or a specific duty.[10]

The EU, Argentina, and Indonesia: Biodiesel

In the previous example, the duties on biodiesel of between 22 and 25.7 percent for Argentina, and between 8.8 and 20.5 percent for Indonesia, are *ad valorem* ADDs.

Mexico and China: Seamless steel pipe

In 2014, Mexico imposed anti-dumping duties of $1,568.92 per metric ton on imports of some categories of seamless steel pipe from China. These were specific ADDs.[11]

3.1.4 Espousal of claims

If a company's products are the object of an anti-dumping investigation, the company can request its home-country[12] government to espouse its claim with the government of the importing country, or, following the imposition of anti-dumping duties, to bring a complaint to the WTO Dispute Settlement Body (DSB).[13]

3.1.4.1 With the government of an importing country

Trade disputes between the government of an importing country and a foreign company[14] can be highly problematic for the company, because the power and legal playing fields are not level.[15] When the company's claim is espoused by its home-country government, this helps to level the playing fields and increases the possibility of a mutually acceptable outcome.

Saudi Arabia and India: Petrochemicals

In January 2014, Saudi Arabia's minister for commerce and industry, Tawfiq Al-Rabiah, said the government of India had dropped its anti-dumping investigation against Saudi-based Chemanol Company—the Kingdom's only exporter of pentaerythritol.

Tawfiq Al-Rabiah said that the ministry's efforts had, in coordination with Chemanol, "helped in ending the investigation launched by the Indian authorities"; that during the investigation, Chemanol was able to show it was not importing the product at less than normal value; that the kingdom had raised the issue at meetings of the Saudi-Indian Joint Commission; and that the Saudi Embassy in New Delhi had coordinated with Indian authorities.[16]

3.1.4.2 *With the WTO Dispute Settlement Body*

If a dispute between a foreign company and the government of an importing country cannot be resolved, the company may opt to have the dispute taken to the WTO DSB. In these situations, the company will need its home-country government to espouse its claim, because the WTO is an intergovernmental organization—and only nation-states and separate customs territories have standing to bring a complaint to the WTO DSB.[17]

The EU and Argentina: Biodiesel

Following the imposition of anti-dumping duties by the EU on biodiesel imports from Argentina and Indonesia in 2013, which is discussed in Section 3.1.3.1, the government of Argentina espoused the claim on behalf of the three Argentine companies and filed a complaint against the EU with the WTO DSB.

3.1.5 *The surrogate third-country rule*

Article VI of the GATT provides that, when determining normal value, "due allowance shall be made in each case for…differences affecting price comparability."

Because of this provision, if the exporting country is not a market economy, the government of the importing country may use a surrogate third country when determining normal value. In these cases, normal value refers to the price at which similar products are sold in the domestic market of the surrogate third country.

China and the EU: CD and DVD products

China's marketization level exceeds the market economy critical level of 60 percent. But when the government of China negotiated the terms of its accession to membership in the WTO (which came into effect in 2001), it agreed to allow WTO members to treat China as a non-market economy in anti-dumping cases until 2016.

In 2005, the EU held anti-dumping investigations into the importation of CD-R and DVD+/−R products from the mainland of China. When determining if these products were imported at less than normal value, the EU used Malaysia as the surrogate third country in the CD-R investigation, and used Taiwan as the surrogate third country in the DVD+/−R investigation.

3.2 Subsidies and countervailing duties

The 1994 WTO Agreement on Subsidies and Countervailing Measures (SCM)[18] defines a subsidy as a "financial contribution by a government or any public body"[19] if the financial contribution benefits "an enterprise or industry or group of enterprises or industries…within the jurisdiction of the granting authority."[20]

The WTO's 2006 World Trade Report says the term *subsidy*, as defined in the SCM, applies only to financial contributions that are made to enterprises or industries located within "a WTO member's own 'territory.'"[21]

3.2.1 Types of subsidies

The types of financial contributions covered by the SCM definition include:

- The direct transfer of funds, such as grants, loans, and equity infusions
- The potential direct transfer of funds, such as loan guarantees
- Government revenue "forgone or not collected," such as tax exemptions and fiscal incentives
- Goods and services provided by the government, other than general infrastructure[22]
- The governmental purchase of products
- Any income or price support that operates directly or indirectly to increase exports of any product from, or reduce imports into, the territory of the granting authority

The SCM definition also includes financial contributions in any of these categories, even if the payment has been made "to a funding mechanism" or through "a private body."[23]

In practice, the provisions contained in the SCM are seen as covering a wide range of governmental financial contributions or other governmental actions that support domestic producers, which include:

- Governmental assistance programs, such as support programs that provide farmers or manufacturers with tax exemptions and tax credits, or with low-interest or interest-free loans
- Governmental measures to support or protect domestic industries, including government-sponsored "buy-national" programs
- Governmental procurement policies (such as preference for domestic products when procuring defense-related products, and in other government purchasing) and government monopolies
- Governmental support for the development of new products, or for the establishment of new industries or new industry segments

The US and the EU: Airbus and Boeing

In 2004, the United States government filed a complaint with the WTO DSB, which claimed Airbus had received subsidies from the European Communities,[24] the EU, and the governments of Germany, France, the United Kingdom (UK), and Spain. The complaint said the subsidies were in the form of loans, grants, equity, and debt forgiveness; were related to the development of large civil aircraft; and totaled more than $22 billion.

The same year, the EU responded by filing a complaint with the WTO DSB, which claimed Boeing had received subsidies from departments and agencies of the United States government;[25] from the state governments of Kansas, Illinois, and Washington; and from municipal governments in these states. The complaint said the subsidies were in the form of tax and non-tax incentives, funding, support, and tax relief and totaled more than $23 billion.

3.2.2 The distortion of free trade

The term *distortion of free trade* refers to actions by governments that interfere with or limit free trade—by restricting imports or supporting exports. The term usually refers to the effects of governmental actions that are less severe than the effects of trade barriers—and usually refers to the indirect or secondary effects of governmental actions.

3.2.2.1 The effect of subsidies on imports

Subsidies can benefit farmers and manufacturers by reducing their production costs, which allows them to reduce the prices at which they market their products domestically. This can distort free trade, because reduced domestic prices make it more difficult for imported products to compete with domestically produced products.[26]

3.2.2.2 The effect of subsidies on exports

Subsidies can also distort free trade because they allow farmers and manufacturers to reduce their production costs—and to reduce the prices at which they export their products.

3.2.3 Prohibited, actionable, and allowed subsidies

Financial contributions by governments and public bodies can be classified as prohibited subsidies, actionable subsidies, or allowed subsidies.

3.2.3.1 Prohibited subsidies

Article 3 of the SCM says subsidies are prohibited if they:

1. Are "contingent...upon export performance."[27] Subsidies in this group, which are commonly referred to as *export subsidies*, are listed in an annex to the SCM.[28]
2. Are "contingent...upon the use of domestic over imported goods."[29] Subsidies in this group are sometimes referred to as *local content subsidies*.[30]

3.2.3.2 Actionable subsidies

Article 5 of the SCM says WTO members should not use any subsidy that will cause "adverse effects" to another WTO member. These adverse effects can be divided into two types.

1. "Injury to the domestic industry of another Member"[31]
   When applied to subsidies, the injury to a domestic industry criterion is similar to the application of this criterion in anti-dumping cases.

2. "Serious prejudice to the interests of another Member"[32]
   The term *serious prejudice* refers to subsidies that can result in the distortion of free trade,[33] and include subsidies that exceed 5 percent of a product's value or that cover operating losses or the forgiveness of debt if the effect of the subsidy (1) displaces or impedes imports, (2) causes significant price suppression in the domestic market, or (3) increases the country's "world market share" of a product.[34]

These contributions are called actionable subsidies, because they can be the object of a countervailing action by another member, or can be the grounds for a complaint to an intergovernmental dispute settlement mechanism[35] such as the WTO DSB.

3.2.3.3 Allowed subsidies

There are two groups of subsidies that are allowed.

1. Contributions that fall outside the SCM definition[36]
   Allowed subsidies include contributions that are related to the development or improvement of general infrastructure (including roads, port facilities, water and gas reticulation, and electricity grids), to non-company-specific and non-industry-specific tax incentives, and to other contributions that do not benefit "an enterprise or industry or group of enterprises or industries."[37]

2. "Non-actionable subsidies"
   Article 8 of the SCM lists some exceptions to the subsidies in the actionable category, which are called *non-actionable subsidies*. These exceptions include "assistance for research activities conducted by firms or by higher education or research establishments,"[38] "assistance to disadvantaged regions within the territory of a Member,"[39] and "assistance to promote adaptation of existing facilities to new environmental requirements."[40] Each of these exceptions is narrowly defined, and each is subject to limitations and conditions.

An allowed subsidy cannot be the object of a countervailing action by another member, and cannot be the grounds for a complaint by another member to an intergovernmental dispute settlement mechanism.

The US and the EU: Airbus and Boeing

A large part of the work done by the WTO DSB panels and Appellant Body, when deciding the Airbus and Boeing complaints filed by the US and the EU in 2004,[41] was to establish the facts and decide issues of law to determine which of the alleged subsidies were actionable.[42] These complaints were the largest cases to have been handled by the WTO DSB, and this work took more than six years to complete.[43]

The 2011 and 2012 Appellate Body reports found that, in both cases, some of the alleged subsidies were allowed and some were actionable. The reports also found that the actionable subsidies had, inter alia, caused serious prejudice to the US and the EU, and had resulted in significant losses in sales by Boeing and Airbus.

3.2.4 *Countervailing duties*

Customs duties that are used to counter the effects of subsidies are referred to as *countervailing duties* (CVDs). In most cases,[44] a CVD is a trade remedy that is applied to products made by a specific company that has benefited from specific governmental financial contributions in a specific exporting country.

3.2.4.1 *The purpose and level of CVDs*

The purpose of a CVD is to nullify the financial benefit that has been contributed by the government (or by governments and/or by a public body) in an exporting country—by adding to the price at which the subsidized product is sold in the importing country.

The US and the EU: Airbus and Boeing

Following the final determinations by the WTO DSB, the US requested authorization from the DSB to impose CVDs of $12 billion annually on Airbus; the EU requested authorization to impose CVDs of $7 billion to $10 billion annually on Boeing.

CVDs are not intended to be punitive, but are intended only to nullify the benefit conferred by a subsidy. Article 19.4 of the SCM says a CVD on an imported product must not exceed "the amount of the subsidy found to exist."

3.2.4.2 *The two-part test*

Before applying CVDs, a governmental investigation must determine: (1) that an imported product has benefited from a subsidy and (2) that this benefit has caused "adverse effects" to another WTO member. Adverse effects can be either "injury to the domestic industry of another Member" or "serious prejudice to the interests of another Member."[45]

In some cases, a governmental investigation determines that a product has benefited from a subsidy, but determines that the subsidy has not caused adverse effects.

The US and China, Ecuador, India, Malaysia, and Vietnam: Shrimp

In August 2013, in response to a petition filed by the US Coalition of Gulf Shrimp Industries, the US Department of Commerce announced that imports of shrimp from China, Ecuador, India, Malaysia, and Vietnam had benefited from governmental subsidies in their countries of origin, and that the department was imposing CVDs on these imports of between 7.8 and 54.5 percent—subject to a review by the US International Trade Commission.

In September 2013, the USITC announced it was rescinding the decision by the Department of Commerce, because "a US industry is neither materially injured nor threatened with material injury by reason of imports of frozen warm water shrimp from China, Ecuador, India, Malaysia, and Vietnam that the US Department of Commerce has determined are subsidized."[46]

It is important to note that, in this case, the USITC did not disagree with the department's finding that the imports were subsidized, and that the USITC's reason for disallowing the imposition of the CVDs was based solely on the absence of adverse effects.

3.2.4.3 Cross-retaliation duties

Most CVDs are applied to products that have benefited from subsidies. In some cases, however, an importing country applies CVDs to products that have not benefited from a subsidy—to countervail against the effects of subsidies on another product. These CVDs are referred to as *cross-retaliation duties*.

The US and Brazil: Cotton

In 2002, the government of Brazil brought a complaint to the WTO DSB against the United States for the annual payment of more than $3 billion in subsidies to cotton farmers. In 2004, a WTO arbitration panel found the US subsidies had injured Brazil.

In 2007, 2008, and 2009, the WTO authorized Brazil to apply several countervailing remedies, including cross-retaliation duties, against a wide range of products (including intellectual property imports) from the United States.

3.3 The politicization of trade barriers

A combination of domestic and international factors can result in the politicization of a national government's authority to regulate trade and investment.

The extraordinary success of the GATT, the WTO, and regional trade blocs has made it difficult for national governments to politicize the use of tariffs. But the latitude provided by the general exceptions contained in Article XX of the GATT, and by the rules contained in the WTO's Agreement on Technical Barriers to Trade,[47] allow for the politicization of NTBs[48] and other trade barriers.

Germany: Electrical tools

The German government's treatment of electrical tools from China (which is discussed in Chapter 2, Section 2.3.1.3) appears to have been influenced by domestic political factors.

The US: Steel

In March 2002, the US government applied safeguard duties of between 8 and 30 percent to some categories of steel entering the United States.[49] The application of these duties appears to have been politically motivated because, during the 2000 presidential campaign, George W. Bush had promised steel workers in West Virginia that, if elected, he would apply these duties.

Developed countries: Agriculture subsidies

One reason some developed countries have refused to discontinue the use of agriculture subsidies is that, in these countries, the voting patterns of farmers make them key political constituencies.[50]

Endnotes

1. GATT, Article VI, 1.
2. The surrogate third-country rule is discussed in Section 3.1.5.
3. The term *country of origin* is discussed in Chapter 2, Section 2.2.3.
4. GATT, Article VI, 1(b)(ii).
5. GATT, Article VI, 1.
6. De Vera, "US Anti Dumping Case." The term *fair value* (rather than *normal value*) is used frequently in the United States, because the Tariff Act of 1930 and the USITC's Antidumping and Countervailing Duty Handbook use the term *less than fair value*.
7. Baldwin, "Anti-Dumping Ruling."
8. Biodiesel is produced from soya beans and soybean oil in Argentina, and from palm oil in Indonesia.
9. Giannoulis, "EU Imposes Anti-Dumping Duties."
10. *Ad valorem* tariffs and specific duty tariffs are discussed in Chapter 2, Sections 2.2.1.3 and 2.2.1.4.
11. About one-third of all recent anti-dumping actions in the world have been against products imported from China.
12. The term *home country* is discussed in Chapter 6, Section 6.1.1.2.
13. The WTO Dispute Settlement Body is discussed in Chapter 9, Section 9.5.
14. These disputes are called disputes between nation-states and nationals of other nation-states, and are discussed in Chapter 9, Sections 9.2.2.3 and 9.3.3.
15. This aspect of trade disputes is discussed in Chapter 9, Section 9.2.4.
16. Ghafour, "KSA Wins Case."

17. The use of the DSB is discussed in Chapter 9, Section 9.5.
18. The SCM is one of the agreements concluded in the Uruguay Round of multilateral trade negotiations. The Uruguay Round is discussed in Chapter 7, Section 7.3.2.2.
19. SCM, Article 1.1(a)(1).
20. SCM, Article 2.1.
21. *World Trade Report 2006*, II.B.3, 54.
22. The general infrastructure exception is discussed in Section 3.2.3.3, Item 1 of this chapter.
23. SCM, Article 1.1(a)(1)(iv).
24. The European Communities were entities that in 1993 became part of the EU.
25. These included the Department of Defense, the Department of Commerce, the Department of Labor, and the National Aeronautics and Space Administration.
26. The effects of subsidies on imports are discussed in Chapter 7, Section 7.6.3.1.
27. SCM, Article 3.1.1.
28. This prohibition exempts subsidies that are "provided in the Agreement on Agriculture."
29. SCM, Article 3.1.2.
30. Local content requirements are discussed in Chapter 2, Section 2.3.2.1, and in Chapter 5, Sections 5.2.2 and 5.3.1.
31. SCM, Article 5.1.
32. SCM, Article 5.3.
33. The distortion of free trade is discussed in Section 3.2.2.
34. These factors are discussed in SCM, Article 6.
35. Intergovernmental dispute settlement mechanisms are discussed in Chapter 9, Section 9.3.1.
36. The SCM definition of a subsidy is provided in Section 3.2.
37. SCM, Article 2.1.
38. SCM, Article 8.2.1.
39. SCM, Article 8.2.2.
40. SCM, Article 8.2.3.
41. These complaints are discussed in Section 3.2.1.
42. The roles of panels and the Appellant Body at the WTO DSB are discussed in Chapter 9, Sections 9.5.2 and 9.5.3.
43. Article 12.8 of the 1994 Understanding provides that "the period in which the panel shall conduct its examination . . . shall, as a general rule, not exceed six months." The 1994 Understanding is discussed in Chapter 9, Section 9.5.
44. The exception is cross-retaliation duties, which are discussed in Section 3.2.4.3.
45. This two-part test is similar to the two-part test used in anti-dumping investigations, which is discussed in Section 3.1.1.
46. USITC, *Frozen Warmwater Shrimp*. In this announcement, the USITC said imports take up 35.7 percent of the US industry, which includes 48 producers and 2,050 workers.
47. Article XX of the GATT and technical barriers to trade are discussed in Chapter 2, Section 2.3.1.
48. Non-tariff barriers are discussed in Chapter 2, Section 2.3.
49. Canada and Mexico were exempted from these duties. The EU, followed by Japan, South Korea, China, Taiwan, Switzerland, and Brazil filed a complaint with the WTO DSB, which, in November 2003, decided against the US and authorized more than $2 billion in sanctions if the duties were not removed. The duties were removed in December 2003.
50. This phenomenon is discussed in Chapter 7, Section 7.6.3.

4 Investment barriers

Contents

4.1 Foreign direct investment

The term *foreign investment* refers to investment that is made in a nation-state by an individual or company that is a national of another nation-state.[1] The term also includes investment by an individual or company that is a national of the nation-state that is the location of the investment, but is a resident of a separate customs territory.[2]

All foreign investment can be classified as either (1) *foreign direct investment* (FDI) or (2) *foreign portfolio investment* (FPI).[3]

In the conduct of international commerce, the term *investment barriers* refers to barriers that restrict or regulate FDI.

4.1.1 Definition

There is no generally accepted definition of foreign direct investment, because the criteria that define FDI are set by the government of each host country.[4] There is, however, a widely used definition that was developed by the Organisation for Economic Co-operation and Development (OECD).[5]

The OECD benchmark defines FDI as "a category of cross-border investment" that is made for the purpose of "establishing a lasting interest in an enterprise."[6]

> The motivation of the direct investor is a strategic long-term relationship with the direct investment enterprise to ensure a significant degree of influence by the direct investor in the management of the direct investment enterprise.

The OECD benchmark also says that "the direct investor owns at least 10 percent of the voting power of the direct investment enterprise." But the principal criteria contained in the OECD benchmark are qualitative: They address the investor's purpose and motivation.

> The main motivation of the direct investor is to exert some degree of influence over the management of its direct investment enterprise, whether or not this entails exercising a controlling interest.
>
> The motivation to significantly influence or control an enterprise is the underlying factor that differentiates direct investment from cross-border portfolio investments.

4.1.1.1 The FPI–FDI dichotomy

The OECD benchmark says that in portfolio investment, "…the investor's focus is mostly on earnings resulting from the acquisition and sales of shares and other securities without expecting to control or influence the management of the assets underlying these investments."

An exception to this focus on earnings is when companies use FPI as an element of their IB strategies. For example, companies that engage in international strategic alliances (ISAs)[7] sometimes acquire FPI equity in their alliance partner—for the primary purpose of strengthening their relationship with their alliance partner. Because a company cannot exercise operational managerial control over portfolio investments, FPIs cannot be used as part of a company's IB operations.[8]

4.1.1.2 The focus on FDI

Investment barriers that apply to FDI do not apply to FPI, and the term *investment* in WTO instruments refers solely to FDI.

For example, references to investment in the 1994 Agreement on Trade-Related Investment Measures (TRIMs),[9] which is part of the body of WTO instruments,[10] are to FDI.

4.1.2 Purposes and processes

The purpose of FDI may be to do product-related research, design, and/or development; to manufacture products; to engage in agriculture; to engage in minerals exploration and/or mining; to market products; to provide customer service; and/or to engage in or support international trade.

The processes used by companies to engage in FDI can be classified as either *build* or *buy*.

4.1.2.1 The build option

A company is using the FDI build option when it incorporates a subsidiary in a foreign country and when it hires employees and acquires offices, factories, machinery, and/or other assets in a foreign country.

The US and Japan: American Honda Motor Co., Inc.

In 1959, Honda (a Japanese corporation) established American Honda Motor Co., Inc. (AHM) as a US affiliate,[11] incorporated in California. The purpose of this company, which was Honda's first overseas subsidiary, was to facilitate the US distribution of motorcycles manufactured by Honda in Japan. AHM, which began with three employees, appointed distributors in the US and outsourced advertising campaigns.

By the early 1990s, Honda was selling twice as many cars in the US as in Japan, and AHM and its sibling and subordinate subsidiaries in the US were performing research, design, development, and manufacturing of components, motor vehicles, and other products in the US. In 2013, Honda became a net exporter of motor vehicles from the US.[12]

4.1.2.2 The buy option

A company is using the buy option to engage in FDI when it acquires a company, or acquires a lasting interest in a company, in a foreign country.

The US, the UK, and the UAE: Dubai Ports World

In 2005, Dubai Ports International (DPI), a United Arab Emirates (UAE) state-owned enterprise with container-shipping terminal assets and operations in the Middle East, Africa, Europe, and India, paid $1.14 billion to acquire CSX World Terminals (CSXWT), a US corporation. This FDI gave DPI ownership of CSXWT and ownership of CSXWT's container-shipping terminal assets and operations in Australia, China, the Dominican Republic, Finland, Germany, Hong Kong, the Netherlands, Puerto Rico, Russia, South Korea, the US, and Venezuela.

In 2006, Dubai Ports World (DPW)[13] paid $6.8 billion to acquire Peninsular and Oriental Steam Navigation Company (P&O), a UK corporation and the world's fourth-largest shipping terminal operator. This acquisition gave DPW ownership of P&O, its operating subsidiaries, its assets, and its 29 container-shipping terminal operations in 18 countries—which included contracts for the management and operation of shipping terminals in Baltimore, Miami, New Jersey, New Orleans, New York, Philadelphia, and 16 other ports in the United States.

4.1.3 Types of FDI barriers

Barriers to FDI can be classified as either entry barriers or post-entry barriers[14] and as either industry specific or non-industry specific.

4.1.3.1 Entry barriers to FDI

The term *entry barriers to FDI* refers to barriers that prevent, restrict, or regulate the entry of FDI into a host country.

Entry barriers to FDI are discussed in the remaining sections of this chapter.

4.1.3.2 Post-entry barriers to FDI

The term *post-entry barriers to FDI* refers to barriers that restrict or regulate the operations of FDI after it has entered a host country.

Post-entry barriers to FDI are discussed in Chapter 5.

4.1.3.3 Industry-specific barriers to FDI

Barriers to FDI can be industry specific, sub-industry specific,[15] or non-industry specific.[16]

The term *industry-specific barriers to FDI* refers to FDI barriers that apply to a single industry. Most entry barriers to FDI are industry specific.

Industry-specific entry barriers to FDI are referred to as *industry access barriers*.

4.2 Industry access barriers

An industry access barrier is an FDI barrier that prevents or restricts a foreign investor from entering a specific industry or industry segment in a host country.[17]

The method that is most widely used by nation-states to prevent or restrict access to an industry is *equity restrictions*, which are also referred to as *ownership restrictions*.

4.2.1 *Equity restrictions*

Equity restrictions limit the percentage of the ordinary issued and outstanding shares that foreign investors are permitted to own in a company in a host country. Equity restrictions can also cover operating conditions.

Industries in host countries can be classified as either closed or open to FDI. Open industries can be classified as either unrestricted or restricted.

4.2.1.1 *Closed industries*

If foreign investors are prohibited from owning equity in a company in a specific industry, this is referred to as *full exclusion*. Fully excluded industries are also referred to as being *closed to FDI*.

Industries that are closed to FDI include the agriculture and forest products industries in Japan; the fishing industries in Brazil, Chile, China, Iceland, Indonesia, Italy, Japan, Saudi Arabia, and the US; the media industry in China; the real estate industries in the Czech Republic, Saudi Arabia, Slovak Republic, and Turkey; the mining industries in Iceland, Japan, and Saudi Arabia; and the electricity generation and distribution industries in Iceland and Austria.

4.2.1.2 *Unrestricted open industries*

If there are no restrictions relating to the foreign ownership of equity in companies in an open industry, the industry is referred to as *unrestricted*.

Unrestricted industries include the manufacturing, oil refining and chemicals, metals and minerals, machinery, electronic and electrical instruments, transportation equipment, electricity generation and distribution, construction, wholesale trade, and retail trade industries in the Czech Republic, Denmark, France, Germany, Hungary, Luxembourg, the Netherlands, Poland, Portugal, Romania, Slovak Republic, Spain, Sweden, and Turkey.

4.2.1.3 *Restricted open industries*

The term *restricted industries* refers to open industries where the amount of foreign equity ownership is limited or is subject to conditions. The most common restrictions limit FDI equity ownership to 50 percent of a company's shares, or prohibit full foreign ownership of a company by requiring a minimum domestic equity ownership.

China: Car manufacturing

In China, the car segment of the automotive manufacturing industry is restricted. Governmental regulations require that equity ownership by foreign investors in car manufacturing companies not exceed 50 percent.[18]

Because of this requirement, most FDI in the automotive industry in China is through equity joint ventures (EJVs). These include the 50–50 EJV between Volkswagen and First Automotive Works, the 40–60 EJV between Volkswagen and Shanghai Automotive Industry Corporation, the 50–50 EJV between Toyota and Guangzhou Automobile Group, and the 50–50 EJV between Honda and Dongfeng Motor.

4.2.2 Operating conditions

Equity ownership restrictions can also include terms and conditions relating to a foreign investor's operations.

China: Car manufacturing for export

The 50 percent equity-ownership restriction that governs FDI in the car segment of the automotive manufacturing industry in China[19] applies to companies that market all or some of their products in China. If all of the vehicles produced by a car manufacturing company are for export, the foreign investor is permitted to own up to 100 percent of the company's equity.

Honda has two EJVs in China with Dongfeng Motor Corporation. One of these EJVs (Dongfeng Honda Automotive Company) manufactures and markets vehicles in China. Honda's equity ownership in this EJV is 50 percent.

Honda's other EJV with Dongfeng (Honda Automobile [China] Company) manufactures vehicles solely for export. Honda's equity ownership in this EJV is 65 percent.

4.3 Reasons for restricting access

There are several reasons governments of nation-states close industries to FDI or apply restrictions to open industries. These reasons include: (a) to protect domestic industries and companies from foreign competition, (b) to protect national security, (c) to protect or achieve national interests, and (d) to protect an industry from unwanted foreign cultural, social, or political influence.

4.3.1 Foreign competition

The reason that drives most industry-access restrictions on FDI is the protection of domestic companies or domestic industries from foreign competition. The underlying rationale for protecting domestic companies and industries from FDI are the same as, or similar to, the rationale for the protectionist use of tariffs and NTBs.[20]

4.3.2 National security

The governments of most nation-states have policies and procedures that restrict FDI that could potentially threaten national security, even if the FDI would be in an open industry.

The US: The CFIUS

The responsibility for deciding if a foreign direct investor poses a threat to US national security rests with the Committee on Foreign Investment in the United States (CFIUS).[21]

The members of this committee represent 12 government departments and agencies: the Treasury; the Departments of State, Defense, Commerce, Homeland Security, and Justice; the Office of Management and Budget; the Council of Economic Advisors; the National Security Council; the National Economic Council; the Office of Science and Technology Policy; and the US Trade Representative.[22] CFIUS is chaired by the Secretary of the Treasury.

The US: DPW and P&O

In 2005, prior to DPW's acquisition of P&O,[23] DPW and P&O contacted CFIUS because P&O operated shipping terminals in Baltimore, Miami, New Jersey, New Orleans, New York, and Philadelphia, and in 16 other US ports—and because the companies believed the "proposed transaction could raise national security issues that should appropriately be reviewed by the US Government."[24]

This initiative was followed by DPW and P&O briefings for CFIUS members, independent analyses by each of the CFIUS member departments and agencies, a request for an intelligence assessment of DPW by CFIUS, and the negotiation of an assurances letter with the companies by the Department of Homeland Security. At the end of the process, on January 17, 2006, "all CFIUS members agreed that this particular transaction should be allowed to proceed."[25]

4.3.3 National interest

In some cases, the reason a national government gives for restricting industry access is the *national interest*. This is an extremely broad term that can include criteria related to economic development, creating or preserving employment, and/or effecting technology transfer.

China: Car manufacturing and technology transfer

One of the reasons for the 50 percent equity-ownership restriction on FDI in car manufacturing companies in China is to facilitate the transfer of manufacturing and managerial technology from foreign-funded companies[26] to Chinese-funded companies.

Because equity joint ventures and other forms of strategic alliances are a highly practical and proven mechanism for effecting technology transfer, the government of China has adopted a policy of encouraging and in some cases

mandating the use of international strategic alliances to achieve China's economic development goals.

4.3.4 Unwanted foreign cultural, social, or political influence

In some cases, governments of nation-states prohibit or restrict industry-specific
FDI—for the purpose of protecting an industry from unwanted foreign cultural,
social, or political influence.

The media industries in China and France

In China, the media industry is closed to FDI; in France, FDI in the media
industry is severely restricted. The reasons appear to be related to these nation-
states wanting to limit foreign cultural, social, or political influence in their
media industries.

4.3.5 Combinations and ambiguity

In some cases, the decision by a national government to prohibit or restrict FDI in an
industry may be motivated by a combination of two or more reasons.

In some nation-states, specific industries are reserved for state-owned enterprises.[27] This reservation may be due to a combination of national security and
national interest reasons, but may also be or influenced by social, cultural, political,
or economic reasons.

It can be difficult to determine the principal reason for some industry-specific
barriers because the government may not give a reason for imposing a restriction, or,
as in the case of NTBs, because it may be a *disguised restriction*.[28]

4.3.6 No or low industry restrictions

Data developed by the OECD show that the most open industries (that is, the industries with no FDI equity-ownership restrictions or the lowest FDI equity-ownership
restrictions) are manufacturing industries.

The reason many developing nation-states impose no or low barriers on foreign
access to manufacturing industries is because of the causal relationship between FDI
in manufacturing and economic development.

FDI in manufacturing:

- Generates investment capital
- Creates employment
- Provides employees with vocational knowledge and skills
- Facilitates the transfer of managerial and manufacturing technology
- Can result in import substitution (which benefits a host-country's balance of
  trade and balance of payments by reducing the need for imports)
- Can result in an increase in exports (which benefits a host-country's balance
  of trade and balance of payments)

The exception to the relative openness of manufacturing industries is those industries that are closed because of national security or are closed or restricted because of national interests.

4.3.7 The politicization of entry barriers

In some cases, the politicization of a national government's regulatory authority can result in the politicization of FDI entry barriers—and the politicized treatment of foreign-funded companies.[29]

The US: DPW and P&O

As discussed in Section 4.3.2, DPW's acquisition of P&O was approved unanimously by the CFIUS. But, because P&O operated shipping terminals at 6 major ports and 16 other ports in the US, and because DPW is a UAE corporation, the acquisition was opposed by some members of the US Congress.

On March 7, 2006, almost two months after the CFIUS completed its review and approved the transaction, DPW and P&O completed the acquisition. On March 8, the House Appropriations Committee voted 62 to 2 to block DPW from acquiring P&O's port operations in the US. On March 9, DPW announced it would divest all of P&O's US port operations.

In December 2006, DPW completed the divestiture of its US port operations to AIG Global Investment Group, the investment subsidiary of American International Group (a US corporation).

The politicization of FDI entry barriers, and the politicized treatment of foreign-funded companies, can be: (1) industry specific, (2) home-country specific, and/or (3) company specific.

The US: DPW and P&O

The arguments in the US media by members of the US Congress indicate that the politicization of DPW's acquisition of P&O was both industry specific and home-country specific. Some of the arguments indicate that, because DPW is a state-owned enterprise, the politicization was also company specific.

When the politicization of a national government's regulatory authority is applied to post-entry barriers to FDI, this results in a phenomenon called *political risk*. Political risk is discussed in Chapter 5, Section 5.5.

4.4 Industry specificity

Most entry barriers to FDI are industry specific, but can also be sub-industry specific and non-industry specific.

4.4.1 Sub-industry specific entry barriers

In some cases, different segments within the same industry have different levels of industry access or have different equity ownership restrictions.

China: Car and car-engine manufacturing

Toyota (a Japanese corporation) has equity joint ventures with several Chinese-funded companies that manufacture and market cars, trucks, and buses—including Guangzhou Automobile Group. The equity ownership in each of these EJVs is 50–50.

Toyota also has a separate EJV with Guangzhou Automobile Group, which manufactures engines that are used in the manufacture of its cars in China, North America, Europe, and Japan. Toyota's equity ownership in this EJV is 70 percent. This is permitted because the 50 percent equity ownership limit in China[30] does not apply to the engine manufacturing segment of the automotive industry.

4.4.2 Non-industry specific entry barriers

Non-industry specific barriers to FDI are barriers that apply to FDI in any and all industries, and to any and all segments or sub-segments within an industry.

4.4.2.1 Minimum investment requirements

Some nation-states have minimum investment requirements, which apply more or less equally to all industries.

Kenya: FDI approval

The government of Kenya says there are no entry barriers for FDI in Kenya. But the approval requirements contained in Kenya's Investment Promotion Act state that, to receive approval from the Kenya Investment Authority, an FDI application must be for not less than US$500,000.

If a foreign company intends to engage in large-scale manufacturing, minimum investment requirements do not act as an entry barrier to FDI.

These requirements can, however, act as an entry barrier to FDI if a company intends to establish small manufacturing operations, to engage in warehousing and/or assembly operations associated with trade, or to enter a service industry or some other non-capital-intensive industry.

4.4.2.2 Other non-industry specific barriers

Non-industry specific barriers to FDI also include currency and financial restrictions and requirements, human resources restrictions and requirements, and land-ownership restrictions. These FDI barriers are discussed in Chapter 5, because they act primarily as post-entry barriers to FDI: They restrict or regulate the operations of FDI after it has entered a host country.[31]

Endnotes

1. Corporate nationality is discussed in Chapter 6, Section 6.1.1.4.
2. Separate customs territories are discussed in Chapter 6, Section 6.1.1.3.
3. Foreign portfolio investment is discussed in Sections 4.1.1.1 and 4.1.1.2. In some countries, foreign portfolio investment is called *foreign indirect investment*.
4. The term *host country* is discussed in Chapter 6, Section 6.1.1.2.
5. The OECD, which was established in 1961, is an intergovernmental organization that has 37 member states. Until recently, the members of the OECD were all economically developed countries.
6. This quotation and all other quotations in Section 4.1.1 are from OECD, *Benchmark Definition of FDI*, Sections 1.4.11 and 2.3.2.29.
7. Strategic alliances and ISAs are discussed in Section 4.3.3 and in Chapter 10, Sections 10.2.2.5, 10.2.3.1, and 10.2.3.2.
8. The term *operations* is defined in Chapter 1, Endnote 1.
9. TRIMs is discussed in Chapter 7, Sections 7.3.2.2, 7.4.3.3, 7.5.2.2, 7.6, and 7.6.1.2.
10. WTO instruments are discussed in Chapter 7, Sections 7.3.2.2 to 7.6.
11. The term *US affiliate* is discussed in Chapter 6, Section 6.1.1.4.
12. In 2013, Honda imported 88,537 vehicles into the US and exported 108,705 vehicles.
13. In 2005, DPI merged with Dubai Ports Authority to become Dubai Ports World.
14. The division between entry and post-entry barriers is also discussed in Chapter 5, Section 5.1.
15. Sub-industry barriers to FDI are discussed in Section 4.4.1.
16. Non-industry specific barriers to FDI are discussed in Section 4.4.2.
17. References to *industry* can also be applied to industry segments and sub-segments.
18. Two exceptions to this requirement are discussed in Sections 4.2.2 and 4.4.1.
19. This restriction is discussed in the example in Section 4.2.1.3.
20. The protectionist uses of tariffs and NTBs are discussed in Chapter 2, Sections 2.2.4.1 and 2.3.1.2.
21. The CFIUS was created by Section 721 of the Defense Production Act of 1950, which is referred to as the Exon-Florio amendment.
22. In some cases, the Departments of Energy and Transportation, the Nuclear Regulatory Agency, and other US agencies participate in CFIUS reviews.
23. DPW's acquisition of P&O is discussed in Section 4.1.2.2.
24. USDOT, Dubai-P&OE-F Fact Sheet.
25. Ibid.
26. The term *foreign-funded company* is discussed in Chapter 6, Section 6.1.1.4.
27. The term *state-owned enterprise* (SOE) refers to a business enterprise that is owned or controlled by the government of a nation-state. In practice, the term is also used when referring to an enterprise that is owned or controlled by a state, provincial, or city government.
28. The term *disguised restriction* is from Article XX of the GATT and is discussed in Chapter 2, Section 2.3.1.3.
29. The politicization of a national government's authority to regulate trade is discussed in Chapter 3, Section 3.3.
30. This equity ownership limit is discussed in Sections 4.2.1.3 and 4.2.2.
31. Currency and financial restrictions and requirements are discussed in Chapter 5, Section 5.2.1. Human resources restrictions and requirements are discussed in Chapter 5, Sections 5.2.3 and 5.3.3.

5 Post-entry barriers

Contents

5.1 Entry and post-entry barriers

The division between entry barriers and post-entry barriers can be applied to both trade barriers and FDI barriers.[1]

5.1.1 Entry and post-entry barriers to trade

All of the tariff barriers and most of the NTBs discussed in Chapter 2 are entry barriers: they restrict or regulate, and in the case of NTBs sometimes prevent, the entry of products into nation-states.

But the anti-dumping duties, subsidies, and countervailing duties discussed in Chapter 3 are post-entry barriers. For example, anti-dumping duties are applied to products after they have been "introduced into the commerce of another country" at less than normal value, and have caused or threaten to cause injury to a domestic industry in the importing country.[2]

5.1.2 Entry and post-entry barriers to FDI

Entry barriers to FDI are discussed in Chapter 4, Sections 4.2 to 4.4.

The term *post-entry barriers to FDI* refers to barriers that restrict or regulate the operations of FDI after it has entered a host country.

5.1.2.1 Classification overlap and ambiguity

The elements of the IB environment discussed in this chapter are post-entry barriers to FDI. These elements can, however, also act as entry barriers to FDI—because they influence a company's decision to invest, or not to invest, in a host country.

Some post-entry barriers to FDI also act as non-tariff barriers to trade, and are the same as or similar to some of the NTBs discussed in Chapter 2, Section 2.3.

And some entry barriers to FDI (such as equity ownership restrictions, and operating conditions related to equity ownership[3]) can act as post-entry barriers to FDI.

5.1.2.2 Non-industry specificity

As discussed in Chapter 4, most entry barriers to FDI are industry specific.[4] Most post-entry barriers to FDI, however, are non-industry specific: They apply to any and all industries, and to any and all segments and sub-segments within a specific industry.

The exceptions are that local-content requirements[5] and political risk post-entry barriers[6] can be industry specific. Also, some non-industry-specific post-entry barriers to FDI, such as land-ownership restrictions,[7] can have industry-specific characteristics—because their effects are especially disadvantageous to FDI in specific industries.

5.1.3 Sources and types of post-entry barriers to FDI

There are four sources and types of post-entry barriers to FDI:

- Legislated barriers
- Contract-specific barriers
- Administrative barriers
- Political risk barriers

5.2 Legislated barriers

Laws that govern FDI operations in a host country, which are created by the legislative branch of the host-country government, can act as post-entry barriers to FDI. Legislated barriers to FDI apply to all foreign-funded companies[8] operating in a host country, unless a law specifically addresses FDI in a particular industry or industry segment.

Legislated barriers include: (1) currency and financial restrictions, (2) local-content requirements, (3) human resources restrictions and requirements, and (4) land-ownership restrictions.

5.2.1 Currency and financial barriers

Currency and financial barriers to FDI can include: (1) restrictions on the convertibility of currencies, (2) restrictions on the repatriation of profits and capital, and (3) other financial operating barriers.

5.2.1.1 Restrictions on the convertibility of currencies

The governments of many nation-states, and especially the governments of developing countries, attempt to limit the outflow of capital by limiting the convertibility of their currencies.

5.2.1.2 Restrictions on the repatriation of profits and capital

The term *repatriation of funds* refers to the remittance of funds from a host country to a foreign investor's home country.[9] In practice, these restrictions prevent funds from leaving the host country and being remitted to any other nation-state. In some cases, restrictions on the repatriation of profits and capital delay, rather than prevent, the international movement of funds.

Some nation-states, and especially developing countries, have laws, rules, and/or regulations that prohibit or limit the repatriation of profits and/or capital.

5.2.1.3 Other financial operating barriers

A company's FDI operations can also be adversely affected by other financial operating barriers. These can include administrative and processing fees or taxes, annual license renewal fees, and taxes on foreign remittances.[10]

5.2.1.4 Barriers to trade

As discussed in Chapter 2, Section 2.3.2.1, Item 1, NTBs include restrictions on payments for imports. Some of the currency and financial restrictions and requirements discussed in this section can, in some cases, also act as NTBs.

5.2.2 Local-content requirements

Local-content requirements can be classified as: (1) legislated local-content requirements and (2) contract-specific local-content requirements.[11]

As discussed in Chapter 4, there are several ways in which FDI in manufacturing can benefit the economic development of a host country.[12] To maximize these benefits, the governments of some host countries have adopted laws that require foreign-funded manufacturers to use not less than a certain level of domestically produced materials and components, and/or to progressively increase the level of local content used in their manufacturing operations.

As discussed in Chapter 2, Section 2.3.2.1, Item 2, local-content requirements can also act as NTBs to trade.

Contract-specific local-content requirements are discussed in Section 5.3.1.

5.2.3 Human resources restrictions and requirements

Human resources (HR) barriers that affect FDI operations can be classified as: (1) legislated HR requirements and (2) contract-specific HR requirements.

Legislated HR requirements are contained in laws that place general restrictions on the employment of foreign nationals[13] and apply to all foreign-funded companies in a host country.

Malaysia: Ethnic employee requirement

Until 2009, Malaysia's New Economic Policy required that foreign-funded companies "allocate 30 percent of their staff positions to ethnic Malays," who make up about 60 percent of the country's population. This requirement was discontinued in 2009, following the implementation of "a new investor-friendly economic model."[14]

In some cases, legislated HR requirements apply to both domestic and foreign-funded companies. These restrictions can, however, be more problematic for foreign-funded companies and their parent companies that need to move managers, executives, and technical personnel between countries where they have operations.

Legislated restrictions can limit the number or percentage of foreign nationals a company is permitted to employ, and/or can limit the number or percentage of foreign nationals who hold positions in specific categories.

The employment of persons who are foreign nationals can be made more complex and difficult because of a host country's application and approval requirements and processes.[15]

Contract-specific HR requirements are discussed in Section 5.3.3.

5.2.4 Land-ownership and leasing restrictions

Some nation-states have laws, rules, and regulations that prevent or restrict the ownership of land by foreign-funded companies.[16] These land-ownership barriers are in most cases not industry specific, but are especially problematic for FDI in some industries.

For foreign-funded companies engaged in agriculture or manufacturing, land-ownership restrictions can severely limit their ability to buy farms or factories, and limit their access to land on which to develop farms or build factories.

Some nation-states that restrict land ownership by foreign-funded companies allow real estate to be leased. But leasing may not be operationally feasible, because a foreign-funded company may be reluctant to invest in improvements to real estate it does not own. The operational feasibility of leasing can be further exacerbated by concerns that, if there is a dispute with a property owner, the property owner may receive preferential treatment by the host-country government and/or by the host country's courts.[17]

In some cases, a host country's laws prohibit foreign-funded companies from leasing land for agricultural use.

Kenya: Land ownership and leasing restrictions

The Kenya Land Control Act prohibits non-citizen enterprises, and joint ventures that include non-citizens, from owning or leasing agricultural land.[18]

5.3 Contract-specific barriers

An FDI agreement is a written contract between a foreign direct investor and the government of a host country.

The terms and conditions contained in a foreign-funded company's FDI agreement can result in post-entry barriers to FDI. These terms and conditions apply only to the FDI that is covered by an agreement, and apply only to the foreign-funded company that is a party to the agreement.

5.3.1 Performance requirements

Agreements between foreign direct investors and the governments of host countries include an almost infinite range of terms and conditions. There is, however, a small group of terms and conditions, called *performance requirements*, that frequently act as post-entry barriers to FDI.

The term *performance requirement* refers to a quantitative level of performance in a specified functional area that must be achieved by an FDI's operations within a specific time period.

Performance requirements can include: (1) local content requirements, (2) export quota requirements, (3) human resources indigenization requirements, and (4) environmental impact requirements.[19]

5.3.1.1 Local-content requirements

As discussed in Section 5.2.2.1, some host-country governments have adopted laws that require foreign-funded manufacturers to use a certain level of domestically produced materials and components.

Some host governments, however, make local-content requirements contract specific—by including local-content schedules in FDI agreements—or by using a combination of legislated and contract-specific local-content requirements.

Local-content schedules require foreign-funded companies, over time, to progressively increase the level of local content used in their manufacturing operations. These schedules usually specify what percentage of the total content value, and what percentage of each category of materials or parts, must be local content by each time milestone specified in the agreement.

5.3.1.2 Export quota requirements

As discussed in Chapter 4, FDI in manufacturing can generate exports, which can benefit a host country's balance of trade and balance of payments.[20]

Some host-country governments attempt to maximize exports by foreign-funded manufacturers by including minimum export quotas in their FDI agreements.[21] Export quota requirements are usually contained in a schedule that specifies the percentage of the foreign investor's output, in each category, that must be exported during each time period covered in the agreement.

5.3.1.3 Human resources indigenization requirements

In the conduct of IB, the term *human resources indigenization* refers to the progressive replacement of employees who are foreign nationals with employees who are host-country nationals.[22]

In host countries that have company-specific indigenization requirements, these requirements are usually contained in an indigenization schedule, which is part of a foreign-funded company's FDI agreement. An indigenization schedule specifies the minimum number or percentage of managers, executives, and technical experts in each category, at each level, who must be host-country nationals (or the maximum number or percentage of allowable foreign nationals)—at each time milestone that is specified in the agreement.

Compliance with indigenization requirements has been problematic for some foreign direct investors, and especially for well-managed companies that have provided advanced levels of training to host-country managers, executives, and technical experts—only to have these employees recruited by other companies or, in some cases, recruited by the host-country government.

5.3.1.4 Environmental impact requirements

The increase in the emphasis on environmental protection has resulted in the governments of some host countries including environmental-impact performance requirements in FDI agreements.

5.3.2 Penalties

The penalties for non-compliance with performance requirements are stated in a host country's FDI laws, rules, and regulations, and/or in specific FDI agreements.

The most serious penalties can include the revocation of a company's FDI approvals by a host country government, which results in the termination of the company's operations in the host country and the partial or total loss of its investment.

5.4 Administrative barriers

The implementation of the laws that govern FDI operations in a host country requires the use of administrative rules and requirements, which are created and administered by the executive branch of the host-country government.

In some cases, administrative rules and requirements, and related decisions and actions, can act as post-entry barriers to FDI.

Administrative barriers include: (1) application and approval requirements and processes, (2) the lack of transparency, and (3) the absence of established procedures.

5.4.1 Application and approval requirements and processes

Some of the least recognized but most problematic post-entry barriers to trade and FDI are governmental application and approval requirements and related processes. These requirements and processes can increase the cost, complexity, and difficulty of operating in a host country.

5.4.2 Transparency

When referring to political and governmental structures, systems, and processes, the term *transparency* refers to openness and the availability of information related to: (1) the criteria used when making decisions and (2) the identity and roles of the government departments and personnel who participate in decision-making processes.

The EU: Decision-related transparency

On its "transparency portal" web page, the EU says decisions affecting European citizens' lives "must be taken as openly as possible. As a European citizen, you have a right to know how the European institutions are preparing these decisions, who participates in preparing them, who receives funding from the EU budget, and what documents are held or produced to prepare and adopt the legal acts. You also have a right to access those documents."[23]

The first function of transparency processes is to facilitate public access to information. Other functions of transparency processes include measures to avoid conflicts of interests by persons who participate in decision-making processes—and measures to ensure that these persons do not act in self-interest.

The lack of transparency is often associated with corruption in government, which can be defined as the abuse of governmental authority or power for personal gain.

5.4.3 Established procedures

In some host countries, there is a tendency for governmental decision-making to be autocratic or arbitrary and to be characterized by an absence of established procedures.

Kenya: Exemptions

As discussed in Endnote 18, the Kenya Land Control Act allows the president of Kenya to grant exemptions to restrictions that prohibit non-citizen enterprises, and joint ventures that include non-citizens, from owning or leasing agricultural land.

But this act and other governmental documents say nothing about the process for applying for an exemption. These documents also say nothing about the criteria that the government and the president will use when assessing exemption applications, and contain no information about the positions or identities of the persons in the government who evaluate exemption applications and advise the president concerning the approval of exemptions.

As with the lack of transparency, the absence of established procedures is often associated with corruption in government.

5.4.4 Barriers to FDI and trade

The lack of transparency and the absence of established procedures can act as entry and post-entry barriers to trade and FDI, because they make it difficult or impossible for managers and executive at foreign-funded companies to know:

- How governmental decisions are made
- What criteria are used in making governmental decisions
- What government departments and personnel participate in the decision-making processes
- What is the specific decision-making role and authority of participating departments and personnel

The lack of transparency and the absence of established procedures are reflected in some of the NTBs associated with administrative rules and requirements, which are discussed in Chapter 2, Section 2.3.2.1.

5.5 Political risk barriers

As discussed in Chapters 3 and 4, the politicization of a government's regulatory authority can result in the politicization of trade barriers and the politicization of entry barriers to FDI.[24]

The politicization of a government's regulatory authority can also result in a post-entry barrier to FDI, which is called *political risk*.

Political risk can be defined as the possibility that the politicization of a government's regulatory authority could result in the politicized treatment of a foreign-funded company, its assets, and/or its operations by the legislative, executive, and/or judicial branches of a host-country government.

Political risk can result in the prejudicial application of FDI barriers, which can adversely affect the survival, success, and sustainability of a foreign-funded company, its operations, and/or its parent company.[25]

5.5.1 Nationalization and expropriation

In the most extreme cases, political risk can result in the nationalization or expropriation of a foreign-funded company, its assets, and/or its FDI operations.

In the conduct of international relations and IB, the terms *nationalization* and *expropriation* both refer to the confiscation of a foreign-funded company, its assets, and/or its FDI operations by a host-country government.

In the case of nationalization, the company's shareholders receive compensation.

Venezuela: AES

In 2007, the government of Venezuela nationalized the in-country assets of AES Corporation (a US national) and acquired the company's 82 percent equity interest in Electricidad de Caracas, Venezuela's largest privately owned electrical power company. Following the nationalization, the government of Venezuela paid AES $740 million in compensation.

In the case of expropriation, the company's shareholders do not receive compensation.

Venezuela: Owens Illinois

In 2010, the government of Venezuela expropriated the in-country glass-making operations of Owens Illinois, a Fortune 500 company and a US national, and paid no compensation.

5.5.2 *Types of political risk exposure*

As with the politicization of entry barriers to FDI,[26] the political risk exposures of foreign-funded companies and their FDI operations can be grouped into three types: (1) industry-specific political risk, (2) home-country specific political risk, and (3) company-specific political risk.

5.5.2.1 *Industry-specific political risk*

Since the adoption of Resolution 1803 on the Permanent Sovereignty over Natural Resources by the General Assembly of the United Nations in 1962, and the rise in economic nationalism in the 1960s and 1970s, the highest levels of industry-specific political risk have occurred in FDI in the oil, gas, and mining industries. Some host-country governments have unilaterally changed the terms and conditions of their FDI agreements with foreign-funded companies in these industries, or have used the threat of nationalization or expropriation to force the renegotiation of FDI agreements.

Bolivia: Oil and gas companies

In 2006, the government of Bolivia announced it had nationalized the country's oil and gas industry, and gave the industry's ten foreign-funded companies (from six home countries) six months to renegotiate their terms of ownership and operations or face expulsion.

5.5.2.2 *Home-country-specific political risk*

When the political risk exposure of a foreign-funded company is influenced by its corporate nationality,[27] this is referred to as home-country-specific political risk.

Venezuela: AES and Owens Illinois

The relations between the United States and Venezuela are contentious and politically and ideologically polarized. Because AES Corporation and Owens Illinois are both US nationals, the nationalization of the in-country assets of AES Corporation and the expropriation of Owens Illinois in Venezuela may have been influenced by home-country-specific political risk.

5.5.2.3 *Company-specific political risk*

When a foreign-funded company's political risk exposure is influenced by its behavior and/or reputation, this is referred to as company-specific political risk.

Venezuela: Owens Illinois

The expropriation of the operations of Owens Illinois, in 2010, by the government of Venezuela, may have been influenced by company-specific political risk. Following the expropriation, President Hugo Chavez said in a televised speech that the company "has exploited workers for years and has destroyed the environment in (the state of) Trujillo…and they have taken away the money of Venezuelans."[28]

5.5.2.4 Combinations

In some cases, such as Owens Illinois in Venezuela, a company's political risk exposure or the actions by a host-country government can be influenced by a combination of two or more types of political risk.

Endnotes

1. This division is discussed in Chapter 4, Section 4.1.3.
2. Anti-dumping duties are discussed in Chapter 3, Section 3.1.
3. These equity restrictions to FDI are discussed in Chapter 4, Section 4.2.
4. FDI industry specificity is discussed in Chapter 4, Sections 4.1.3.3 and 4.4.
5. Local-content requirements are discussed in Sections 5.2.2 and 5.3.1.
6. Industry-specific political risk is discussed in Section 5.2.1.
7. Land-ownership restrictions are discussed in Section 5.2.4.
8. The term *foreign-funded company* is discussed in Chapter 6, Section 6.1.1.4.
9. The terms *host country* and *home country* are discussed in Chapter 6, Section 6.1.1.2.
10. Administrative barriers are discussed in Section 5.4.
11. The use of local-content and export quota requirements by WTO members is restricted by Article XI, General Elimination of Quantitative Restrictions, of the GATT, and by the provisions of the Agreement on Trade-Related Investment Measures. These instruments are discussed in Chapter 7.
12. These benefits are discussed in Chapter 4, Section 4.3.6.
13. An individual who is not a host-country national can be referred to as a *foreign national*. The term *host-country national* is discussed in Chapter 6, Section 6.1.1.2. Individual and corporate nationality is discussed in Chapter 6, Section 6.1.1.4. Employees who are foreign nationals can also be referred to as non-nationals, and are commonly referred to as expatriate employees or simply expatriates.
14. Associated Press, "Malaysia Relaxes Investment Rules."
15. Application and approval requirements and processes are discussed in Section 5.4.1.
16. In developing countries, many of these laws, rules, and regulations date from the Mexican Constitution of 1917 and Mexico's land reform program, the adoption of Resolution 1803 on the Permanent Sovereignty over Natural Resources by the General Assembly of the United Nations in 1962, and the rise in economic nationalism that began in the early 1960s.
17. The possibility of host-country nationals receiving preferential treatment in IB disputes is discussed in Chapter 9, Section 9.2.4.2.
18. The Kenya Land Control Act provides, however, that the president of Kenya can grant exemptions to these restrictions. This exemption is discussed in Section 5.4.3.
19. The restrictions on the use of local-content and export quota requirements by WTO members, which are discussed in Endnote 11, also apply to contract-specific local-content and export quota requirements.
20. These benefits are discussed in Chapter 4, Section 4.3.6.

21. Quotas are discussed in Chapter 2, Section 2.3.2.2.
22. The terms *foreign national* and *host-country national* are discussed in Endnote 13.
23. European Commission, EU Transparency Portal.
24. The politicization of trade barriers is discussed in Chapter 3, Section 3.3; the politicization of entry barriers to FDI is discussed in Chapter 4, Section 4.3.7.
25. Davies, "Beyond the Earthquake Allegory"; and Davies, "Political Risk Management."
26. The politicization of entry barriers to FDI is discussed in Chapter 4, Section 4.3.7.
27. Corporate nationality is discussed in Chapter 6, Section 6.1.1.4.
28. Hernandez. "Venezuela's Chávez Orders Expropriation."

Section III

Facilitating elements

6 An introduction to intergovernmental instruments and mechanisms

Contents

6.1 The nation-state

In the conduct of international relations (IR), there is no generally agreed upon definition of the term *nation-state*. The declarative theory of statehood says a state has four essential characteristics: (1) a defined territory, (2) a permanent population, (3) an established government, and (4) the capacity to engage in relations with other states. The constitutive theory of statehood says there is a single essential criterion: recognition by other states.

6.1.1 Related terms and definitions

In the conduct of IR, the terms *state*, *sovereign state*, and *nation-state* tend to be used interchangeably. The terms *sovereign state* and *nation-state* refer to a state, but emphasize the concept of sovereignty.[1] Some intergovernmental instruments[2] (such as the Charter of the United Nations) use the term *state*, but the most widely used of these technical terms is nation-state.

Many nation-states use the term *state* when referring to their territorial sub-units.[3] One reason for the wide usage of the term *nation-state*, instead of the term *state*, is to avoid ambiguity.

6.1.1.1 Nation

In the conduct of IR and IB, the term *nation* (and its use in derivative terms such as *national government*, *member nations*,[4] the *United Nations*, and *international*) is the same as the term *state*. For example, some WTO instruments,[5] such as the Agreement Establishing the WTO,[6] use the terms *nation* and *national* when referring to states or nation-states.

In some academic disciplines, including sociology and anthropology, the term *nation* refers to a community of people that shares a common language, culture, ethnicity, descent, and history—such as the Cherokee Nation.[7] In these disciplines, the term *nation-state* refers to a state where the boundaries are coterminous with the national or ethnic identity of its population. These meanings do not apply to the general usage of the terms *nation*, *national*, and *nation-state* in the conduct and study of IR and IB.

6.1.1.2 Country

Some intergovernmental instruments (such as the GATT, the Agreement Establishing the WTO, and the Agreement on Rules of Origin) use the word *country*, which is a widely used general term for state, sovereign state, nation-state, and nation. The word *country* is also used in some technical terms, which include: country of origin,[8] exporting country, importing country, home country, and host country.

1. Exporting country and importing country:
    The terms *exporting country* and *importing country* are specific to trade.
        The term *exporting country* refers to the nation-state from which a

product is exported. The term *importing country* refers to the nation-state into which a product is imported.

2. Home country and host country

    The term *home country* can be applied to both individuals and companies, and to both trade and investment. The term refers to the nation-state where an individual or a company is a national.[9]

    The term *host country* is specific to investment, and is used primarily when referring to the nation-state that is the location of a foreign-funded company.[10]

    The terms *home country* and *host country* can be used with the term *national* (*home-country national* and *host-country national*) when referring to an individual or a company. An individual or company that is not a host-country national can be referred to as a *foreign national*.[11]

6.1.1.3 Separate customs territory

The Agreement Establishing the WTO uses the terms *state, country, nation*, and *separate customs territory*. Article XII of the agreement defines a "separate customs territory" (SCT) as an entity "possessing full autonomy in the conduct of its external commercial relations."

There are three types of SCTs: (1) customs unions[12] (such as the EU) that include several or many nation-states, (2) territories of nation-states, and (3) independent territories.

The US: SCTs

American Samoa, Guam, Northern Mariana Islands, the US Minor Outlaying Islands, and the US Virgin Islands are territories of the United States and are SCTs.

The WTO: SCT members

There are four SCTs that are members of the WTO: the EU (1995), Hong Kong (1995), Macao (1995), and Taiwan (2002).[13]

In the conduct of international commercial relations, references to states or nation-states include SCTs—and many of the rights and duties of states also apply to SCTs. Also, references to nationals of nation-states include nationals or residents of separate customs territories.

6.1.1.4 Corporate nationality

Determining the nationality of an individual who is a foreign investor is not difficult, because his or her nationality is defined by their citizenship. Determining the nationality of a company, which is referred to as *corporate nationality*, can be more problematic because there is no generally agreed upon single test for corporate nationality.

The criteria that define corporate nationality are set by the government of each host country.[14] The most widely used criteria are: (1) the nation-state within which a company is incorporated, (2) the nationality of a company's principal shareholders, (3) the nationality of the company's major sources of funding, (4) the nation-state within which the company has its principal administrative offices, and (5) the nation-state within which the company has its principal operations.

If the nationality of a company's incorporation is different from the nationality of its principal shareholders, it can generally be referred to as a *foreign-funded company*. The governments and media in different countries, however, use a range of different terms when referring to these companies.

The US: Affiliates

In the US, if a company's incorporation is domestic and the nationality of its principal shareholders is foreign (such as American Honda Motor Co., Inc.,[15] which is incorporated in the US and has a Japanese company as its principal shareholder), the company is called a *US affiliate* or a *US affiliate of a foreign company*. If the nationality of a company's principal shareholders is domestic and its incorporation is foreign (such as Apple Operations International, which has a US company as its principal shareholder and is incorporated in Ireland), the company is called a *foreign affiliate* or a *foreign affiliate of a US parent company*.

6.1.2 Sovereignty

The concept of sovereignty has two dimensions:

1. The *internal dimension* provides that a national government has authority over everything that occurs within the territorial borders of its nation-state.
2. The *external dimension* provides that a national government has the right to represent its nation-state in relations with other nation-states—and the duty not to intervene in the internal affairs of other nation-states.

6.1.2.1 The origin of the concept

The term *sovereignty* was first defined by the French philosopher Jean Bodin. In *De la république*, written in 1576, Bodin argued that the only way to ensure order in society was for the rulers and ruled to be integrated into a single body, and for this body to have absolute authority within a territory. Bodin called this concept *souveraineté*.

6.1.2.2 Europe in the seventeenth century

The concept of sovereignty, as it is applied in the conduct of IR, originated in Europe in the seventeenth century.

Before 1648, most states in Europe were part of a complicated system that divided political authority between local rulers (the princes and kings) and the Pope, who was head of the Catholic Church and the Holy Roman Empire. In most cases, the local rulers exercised authority over secular areas; the Catholic Church exercised authority over religious and ecclesiastical issues.[16]

It was not unusual, however, for local princes and kings to claim they had authority over the appointment of clergy and other religious matters; and in most states the Church controlled land that it taxed and defended, and was involved in other secular matters.

These competing claims of authority led to numerous wars between states and the Holy Roman Empire. The last of these wars ended with the Peace of Westphalia in 1648.

6.1.2.3 The Peace of Westphalia

The Peace of Westphalia[17] was a series of treaties. These treaties were not uniform; they did not define a new system; and they did not refer to the concept of sovereignty. But the Westphalia treaties are seen as having originated the use of the concept of sovereignty—and as having established the principles of sovereignty—in the conduct of international relations. There are several reasons for this.

First, some of the Westphalia treaties (especially those with the Netherlands and Switzerland) granted rulers of a territory supreme authority over all matters (both temporal and religious) within their borders. This established the internal dimension of sovereignty.

Second, some of the treaties (especially those with the German states) granted individual states the right to form alliances with states outside the Holy Roman Empire. This established the external characteristic of sovereignty relating to the authority of national governments in the conduct of international relations.

Third, the treaties denied the Holy Roman Empire the power to intervene in the internal affairs of a nation-state. This established the external characteristic of sovereignty relating to non-intervention in the internal affairs of states.

And finally, because the Westphalia treaties removed religion as a criterion for the division of authority, the only defining characteristic that remained was territory. This established the principle that the concept of sovereignty relates solely to a nation-state's geographical territory.

6.1.2.4 The partial surrender of sovereignty

When a nation-state enters into a treaty or agreement with one or more other nation-states, in most cases it is agreeing to give up part of its sovereignty. This is referred to as the *partial surrender of sovereignty*.[18]

Russia: The ratification[19] of WTO instruments

In 2012, Russia ratified about 60 WTO instruments and acceded to membership in the WTO. In ratifying these instruments, Russia was surrendering part of its sovereignty, because the commitments contained in these instruments limited Russia's freedom on a wide range of issues related to international trade, and required Russia to modify many of its trade-related laws.

6.2 The intergovernmental elements

The term *intergovernmental elements* refers to elements of the IB environment that are created and controlled by the governments of two or more nation-states,[20] for the purpose of achieving economic, political, security-related, social, cultural, or other mutually beneficial goals.

Intergovernmental elements of the IB environment include:

- General Agreement on Tariffs and Trade
- World Trade Organization[21]
- European Union, the ASEAN Free Trade Area, and the North American Free Trade Area[22]
- Hundreds of bilateral free trade areas, and thousands of bilateral trade and investment agreements[23]
- Instruments and mechanisms for the harmonization of laws and mechanisms for the settlement of IB disputes, which include the International Center for the Settlement of Investment Disputes (ICSID) and the Dispute Settlement Body of the WTO[24]

6.2.1 The effects of the intergovernmental elements

The trade and investment barriers discussed in Chapters 2 to 5, which are applied by the governments of single nation-states, restrict or regulate the conduct of IB.

The intergovernmental elements discussed in this chapter, and in Chapters 7 to 9, facilitate the conduct of IB.

The intergovernmental elements of the IB environment:

- Reduce or eliminate barriers to international trade and foreign investment
- Provide the conceptual, structural, and legal parameters that govern or influence the policies, laws, rules, regulations, decisions, and actions of single nation-states
- Govern or influence how the governments of single nation-states treat companies engaged in the conduct of IB
- Harmonize the conflict of laws that affect the conduct of IB
- Facilitate the settlement of IB-related disputes

6.2.2 Primary classifications

6.2.2.1 Instruments and mechanisms

The intergovernmental elements can be classified as either instruments or mechanisms.

- Intergovernmental instruments are discussed in Section 6.3.
- Intergovernmental mechanisms are discussed in Section 6.4.
- Intergovernmental instruments and mechanisms are discussed in Section 6.5.

6.2.2.2 Unilateral, bilateral, and multilateral

Intergovernmental instruments and mechanisms can be classified by their number of participants:

1. *Unilateral* indicates participation in an instrument, such as a declaration, by a single nation-state.
2. *Bilateral* indicates participation in an instrument or mechanism by two nation-states.
3. *Multilateral* indicates participation in an instrument or mechanism by three or more nation-states.

6.2.2.3 Global and regional

Intergovernmental instruments and mechanisms can be classified as either global or regional.

1. *Global*: The term *global* refers to something that occurs or is present in all parts of the world, is applicable to or in all parts of the world, and/or is the same in all parts of the world.
2. *Regional*: The term *region* refers to a geographical sub-area that has definable characteristics. In the conduct of IR and IB, the term *regional* refers to a geographical area or sub-area of the world.

When applied to intergovernmental instruments and mechanisms, the terms *global* and *regional* can refer to geographical participation, geographical scope, and/or to geographical areas of interest, application, or influence.

- The global elements of the IB environment are discussed in Chapter 7.
- The regional elements of the IB environment are discussed in Chapter 8, Sections 8.1 to 8.4.

6.3 Intergovernmental instruments

The term *instrument* is a technical term that covers all written agreements. Intergovernmental instruments are written agreements between nation-states.

6.3.1 The purpose and effects of intergovernmental instruments

On matters related to international commerce, intergovernmental instruments allow nation-states to state and agree to terms and conditions that govern the conduct of IB.

In the IB environment, intergovernmental instruments:

- Provide the legal and operational framework of the IB environment
- Contain the concepts, principles, rules, and requirements that regulate the behavior of nation-states related to the conduct of IB
- Provide nation-states with the means to establish, record, and preserve their rights and duties with other nation-states related to the conduct of IB
- Provide nation-states with the means, and the legal and procedural frameworks, for the creation and operation of international mechanisms
- Facilitate transparency in the IB environment[25]

6.3.2 Treaties and agreements

In the conduct of IR, intergovernmental instruments are divided into two primary categories: treaties and agreements.[26]

> The *treaties* category includes: treaties, charters, conventions, covenants, statutes, and protocols.
> The *agreements* category includes: agreements, declarations, memoranda of understanding (MOUs), modus vivendi, and communiqués.[27]

Each type of instrument in each category has particular applications. There are, however, no rules governing which type of instrument must be used in a particular situation. Also, the United Nations Treaty Handbook says that "the title and form of a document…are less important than its content in determining whether it is a treaty or international agreement,"[28] which allows nation-states considerable latitude when choosing the operative term to use in the title of an instrument.

Despite this allowance for latitude, terms from the treaties category are usually reserved for titles of instruments that have a high level of importance. Also, treaties and other instruments in the treaties category are more often used as global and multilateral instruments. Agreements and other instruments in the agreements category are more often used as regional and bilateral instruments.

6.3.3 Acceptance procedures

The most significant difference between treaties and agreements relates to acceptance procedures. The term *acceptance* or *acceptance procedure* refers to the decisions and actions that must be taken by a nation-state for it to become a party to an instrument.

6.3.3.1 Ratification

In most cases, acceptance for an instrument in the treaties category that has not entered into force is a two-step process. The first step is called *simple signature*. Simple signature is not binding, but indicates a nation-state's intention to commit to the treaty.

The second step is ratification. The term *ratification* refers to the adoption of a resolution by the government of a nation-state that demonstrates "its willingness to undertake the legal rights and obligations contained in the treaty."[29] Ratification also requires that treaty and approval documents be exchanged (in the case of bilateral treaties) or deposited with the designated depository (in the case of multilateral treaties).

Canada, the US, and Mexico: NAFTA

The North American Free Trade Agreement, which created the North American Free Trade Area,[30] was signed by the leaders of Canada, Mexico, and the US in December 1992. Ratification of the agreement by the legislatures of the three countries took until December 1993. Following the "exchange of written notifications certifying the completion of necessary legal procedures,"[31] the agreement entered into force on January 1, 1994.

The GCC–Singapore FTA

In 2008, the member states of the Gulf Cooperation Council (GCC)[32] signed a free trade agreement with Singapore. Because of the delayed ratification by one GCC member, the agreement did not enter into force until 2012.

6.3.3.2 Accession

In most cases, the acceptance procedure for an instrument that has entered into force is referred to as *accession*.[33] The UN *Treaty Handbook* says that "Accession has the same legal effect as ratification."[34] The requirements for accession are the same as for ratification, except that accession is not preceded by simple signature.

Russia: Accession to membership in the WTO

In December 2011, after 18 years of negotiations, the members of the WTO agreed to admit the Russian Federation to full membership. Russia's Protocol of Accession, the GATT, and about 60 other WTO instruments were ratified by the State Duma on July 10, 2012, and by the Federal Council of Russia on July 18.[35] On July 21, "President Vladimir Putin signed into law Parliamentary legislation bringing Russia's trading laws into compliance with the international standards set under the WTO."[36]

The instruments and approval documents were then deposited with the United Nations Secretariat in New York, and membership became effective on August 22, 2012.[37]

The term *ratification* is sometimes used as a general term when referring to either ratification or accession.

6.3.3.3 Definitive signature

In most cases, the acceptance procedure for instruments in the agreements category does not require ratification or accession. For these instruments, "states can express their consent to be legally bound solely upon signature"[38]—using a single-step procedure called *definitive signature*.

Definitive signature requires that an instrument be signed by a person who holds full powers. The term *full powers* refers to the head of state, the head of government, or the minister of foreign affairs of a nation-state—or a person who has been given full powers by a nation-state to represent it on all matters related to a particular treaty or agreement.

6.3.3.4 Exceptions and inconsistencies

In most cases, treaties require ratification, and agreements do not require ratification. There are, however, exceptions this general rule. This is because the choice of acceptance procedure is not governed by the term *treaty* or *agreement* in an instrument's title—but is governed by the terms of acceptance that are contained in the instrument. An instrument's terms of acceptance are usually found near the end of the instrument, under the heading *acceptance*.

If there is an inconsistency between the term in the title of an instrument and the acceptance procedure contained in the instrument, acceptance is governed by the terms contained in the instrument.

The Agreement Establishing the WTO: Ratification

The Agreement Establishing the WTO has the word *agreement* in its title. But this agreement requires ratification, because Article XII: Accession (which governs new membership in the WTO) says that "any state or separate customs territory possessing full autonomy in the conduct of its external commercial relations…may accede to this agreement."

NAFTA and the GCC–Singapore FTA

The instruments creating NAFTA and the GCC–Singapore FTA, which are discussed in Section 6.3.3.1, included the term *agreement* in their titles. But the acceptance procedures in both agreements required ratification.

The titles of subordinate instruments of constitutional treaties frequently include one of the terms from the agreements category, even if the subordinate instrument requires ratification. This is done to indicate that it is a subordinate instrument of a constitutional treaty.

6.4 Intergovernmental mechanisms

Intergovernmental mechanisms are created and maintained by the governments of two or more nation-states. The term *mechanism* is a technical term that covers a range of organizational and functional entities.

6.4.1 Organizational mechanisms

An organizational mechanism is an institutional entity that has a secretariat, an administrative and operational structure, officers, employees, and physical facilities.

6.4.1.1 IR organizational mechanisms

Organizational mechanisms that facilitate the conduct of IR include:

- United Nations organization (UN)
- World Health Organization (WHO)
- International Court of Justice (ICJ) (which is commonly referred to as the World Court)
- Association of Southeast Asian Nations (ASEAN)
- Shanghai Cooperation Organization (SCO)

6.4.1.2 IB organizational mechanisms

Organizational mechanisms that facilitate the conduct of IB include:

- World Trade Organization
- World Customs Organization (WCO)
- World Intellectual Property Organization (WIPO)
- European Union
- ASEAN Free Trade Area
- International Center for the Settlement of Investment Disputes
- United Nations Commission on International Trade Law (UNCITRAL)
- International Institute for the Unification of Private Law (UNIDROIT)
- Hague Conference on Private International Law (HCCH)

6.4.2 Functional mechanisms

A functional mechanism is an entity that performs a specific task or function.

6.4.2.1 IR functional mechanisms

Functional mechanisms that facilitate the conduct of international relations include:

- Security Council of the United Nations
- Six-Party Talks
- MOUDC (the Memorandum of Understanding on Drug Control), which is a sub-regional multilateral functional mechanism that was created to fight the production, trafficking, and use of drugs in the Greater Mekong Subregion

6.4.2.2 *IB functional mechanisms*

Functional mechanisms that facilitate the conduct of IB include:

- WTO Dispute Settlement Body
- MFN provision of the GATT
- NAFTA
- Canada–EU Comprehensive Economic and Trade Agreement (CETA)[39]
- Hundreds of other multilateral and bilateral free trade areas[40]
- Thousands of bilateral trade and investment agreements[41]

6.4.2.3 *Logistical support*

Some functional mechanisms are sub-units of organizational mechanisms: The WTO Dispute Settlement Body[42] and the MFN provision of the GATT[43] are functional sub-units of the WTO. In each of these cases, the organizational mechanism provides logistical support for the functional mechanism.[44]

The logistical support for other functional mechanisms, such as bilateral free trade areas, is provided by government departments or agencies of the nation-states that have created the mechanism.

6.4.2.4 *Evolution*

In some cases, functional mechanisms become organizational mechanisms. For example, the Hague Conference on Private International Law (HCCH) was created as a functional mechanism in 1893, and in 1955 it became an intergovernmental organization;[45] the Shanghai Five Mechanism was created as a functional mechanism in 1996, and in 2001 it became the Shanghai Cooperation Organization.[46]

6.4.3 **The purpose and effects of intergovernmental mechanisms**

In the conduct of IR, intergovernmental mechanisms allow nation-states to implement the provisions of intergovernmental instruments and to achieve intergovernmental policy, strategic, and operational goals.

In the conduct of international commerce, intergovernmental mechanisms

- Provide the organizational, operational, and administrative structures and systems that are used to implement the concepts, principles, and requirements contained in intergovernmental instruments
- Provide forums that facilitate the proposal, deliberation, discussion, drafting, development, and adoption of amendments to existing intergovernmental instruments, and the creation of new intergovernmental instruments
- Influence the decisions, actions, and behaviors of nation-states related to the regulation of international trade and foreign investment—and related to the treatment of companies engaged in the conduct of IB

- Provide the organizational, operational, and administrative structures and systems that facilitate the settlement of international commercial disputes
- Facilitate transparency in the IB environment

6.5 Intergovernmental instruments and mechanisms

6.5.1 Relationships

There are four essential symbiotic relationships between multilateral intergovernmental instruments and multilateral intergovernmental mechanisms.

1. Instruments create mechanisms. The Agreement Establishing the WTO created the WTO.[47]
2. Instruments provide the concepts, principles, and legal parameters that govern the IB environment—and that govern the administration and operations of mechanisms. The Agreement Establishing the WTO; the GATT 1994, GATS, TRIPS, and TRIMs instruments;[48] the Agreement on Rules of Origin;[49] and other WTO instruments provide concepts, principles, rules, requirements, and legal parameters that govern the IB environment. These instruments also govern the administration and operations of the WTO and its subsidiary bodies.
3. Mechanisms facilitate the amendment of existing instruments. The WTO provides a forum for the proposal, deliberation, discussion, drafting, and adoption of amendments to the GATT 1994 instrument and other WTO instruments.
4. Mechanisms facilitate the creation of new instruments. The WTO provides a forum for the proposal, deliberation, discussion, drafting, and adoption of new global, regional, and bilateral intergovernmental instruments that facilitate the conduct of IB.

There are also various combinations of relationships between IR and IB instruments and mechanisms. These can be seen in many of the situations discussed in Chapters 7, 8, and 9.

6.5.2 Relative visibility and importance

Intergovernmental instruments are relatively obscure, whereas intergovernmental mechanisms are relatively visible.

For example, there are frequent references in the media to the WTO, and we often see media images of national leaders attending meetings of intergovernmental organizations. But we rarely see references in the media to the GATT, GATS, TRIPS, or TRIMs instruments, or to other WTO instruments, and we only occasionally see references to trade and investment treaties that have been signed and later ratified by national governments.

This relative visibility does not reflect the relative importance of intergovernmental instruments and mechanisms. Intergovernmental mechanisms provide the organizational and operational elements of the IB environment that facilitate the conduct of IB.

It is the relatively obscure intergovernmental instruments, however, that provide the legal and operational framework of the IB environment, and that prescribe the concepts, principles, rules, and requirements that govern and facilitate the conduct of IB.

Endnotes

1. Sovereignty is discussed in Section 6.1.2.
2. The term *intergovernmental instrument* is discussed in Sections 6.2.2 and 6.3.
3. The nation-states that use the term *state* when referring to their sub-units include Australia, Austria, Brazil, Germany, India, Malaysia, Mexico, Micronesia, Nigeria, Saint Kitts, Somalia, South Sudan, Sudan, the United States, and Venezuela.
4. The 1967 ASEAN Declaration refers to Member Nations. The 2008 ASEAN Charter refers to Member States. ASEAN is discussed in Chapter 8, Sections 8.1 to 8.3; and in Chapter 9, Sections 9.3.1.3 and 9.4.3.
5. WTO instruments are discussed in Chapter 7, Sections 7.3.2.2 to 7.6.
6. The Agreement Establishing the WTO is discussed in Chapter 7, Sections 7.3.2.2 and 7.4.
7. "The very term 'nation,' so generally applied to them [Indian Nations], means 'a people distinct from others'." US Supreme Court, Worcester v. Georgia (1832) page 31 U.S. 519.
8. The term *country of origin* is discussed in Chapter 2, Section 2.2.3.
9. Individual and corporate nationality is discussed in Section 6.1.1.4.
10. The term foreign-funded company is discussed in Section 6.1.1.4.
11. The term *foreign national* is discussed in Chapter 5, Endnote 13.
12. Customs unions are discussed in Chapter 8, Section 8.4.
13. Membership of SCTs in the WTO is discussed in Chapter 7, Section 7.4.2.1.
14. In some cases, different departments of a national government (such as the US Treasury and the US Department of Commerce) use different criteria for determining corporate nationality.
15. AHM is discussed in Chapter 4, Section 4.1.2.
16. Religious issues include theological beliefs and ideology. Ecclesiastical issues include the appointment of clergy and the administration of the church and its land and buildings.
17. Westphalia was a province in what is now Germany.
18. Examples of the partial surrender of sovereignty can be found in Chapter 8, Sections 8.1.1, 8.3, and 8.4.2.
19. Ratification and accession are discussed in Sections 6.3.3.1 and 6.3.3.2.
20. In the conduct of international commercial relations, references to states or nation-states include separate customs territories. This is discussed in Section 6.1.1.3.
21. The GATT, the WTO, and other global intergovernmental elements are discussed in Chapter 7.
22. The EU, the ASEAN Free Trade Area, NAFTA, and other regional intergovernmental elements are discussed in Chapter 8, Sections 8.1 to 8.4.
23. Bilateral intergovernmental elements are discussed in Chapter 8, Sections 8.5 and 8.6.
24. The harmonization of laws and the settlement of international commercial disputes are discussed in Chapter 9.

25. Transparency is discussed in Chapter 5, Section 5.4.2.
26. The UN Vienna Convention refers to the *agreements* category as *international agreements*.
27. Information concerning types of treaties and agreements can be found in the Treaty Reference Guide.
28. UN, Treaty Handbook, Section 5.3.2, Form.
29. UN, Treaty Handbook, Section 3.3.1, Introduction.
30. Free trade areas are discussed in Chapter 8, Sections 8.2.3 and 8.3. NAFTA is discussed in Chapter 8, Sections 8.2, 8.2.2, 8.3.1.6, and 8.3.2.
31. NAFTA, Free Trade Agreement, Article 2203: Entry into Force.
32. The GCC is discussed in Chapter 8, Sections 8.1 and 8.4.1.
33. If a nation-state is one of the founding signatories to a treaty that requires ratification, or becomes a signatory to the treaty before it enters into force, and approves the treaty after it has entered into force, the action of approving the treaty is referred to as ratification, not accession.
34. UN, Treaty Handbook, Section 3.3.4, Accession.
35. The State Duma and the Federal Council of Russia are the lower and upper houses of Russia's parliament: the Federal Assembly of Russia.
36. Press release, Russia's WTO accession ratification.
37. The Russian Federation became the 156th member of the WTO.
38. UN, Treaty Handbook, Section 3.1.4, Definitive signature.
39. The CETA is discussed in Chapter 2, Section 2.3.2.2; and in Chapter 8, Section 8.4.1.
40. Multilateral free trade areas are discussed in Chapter 8, Section 8.3; bilateral free trade areas are discussed in Chapter 8, Section 8.6.
41. Bilateral trade and investment agreements are discussed in Chapter 8, Section 8.5.
42. The Dispute Settlement Body of the WTO is discussed in Chapter 9, Section 9.5.
43. The MFN provision of the GATT is discussed in Chapter 7, Section 7.5.1.
44. The term *logistical support* covers a wide range of facilities and functions, which can included offices and office equipment, administrative services, and staff.
45. The HCCH is discussed in Chapter 9, Section 9.1.4.2.
46. The Shanghai Five Mechanism and the Shanghai Cooperation Organization are discussed in Chapter 8, Section 8.1.2.
47. The Agreement Establishing the WTO is discussed in Chapter 7, Sections 7.3.2.2 and 7.4.
48. These instruments are discussed in Chapter 7, Sections 7.3.3.2 to 7.6.
49. The Agreement on Rules of Origin is discussed in Chapter 2, Section 2.2.3.2.

7 The GATT, the WTO, and other global instruments and mechanisms

Contents

7.1 The GATT and the WTO

The dominant facilitating instruments in the IB environment are the General Agreement on Tariffs and Trade and other WTO instruments. The dominant facilitating mechanism is the WTO.

This is due to several factors. First, the geographical scope of the GATT, other WTO instruments, and the WTO—and their geographical areas of interest, application, and influence—are global.[1]

The second factor is participation: GATT parties, other WTO-instrument parties, and WTO members include more than 80 percent of the world's nation-states (or 95 percent if WTO observers are included)[2] and account for about 98 percent of the world's trade.[3]

A third factor is the length of time the GATT instrument and the WTO (and its predecessor GATT organization) have been in operation. Fourth, they were established as a plus-sum game.[4] And finally, the GATT, other WTO instruments, and the WTO cover most of the operational areas that are critical to the conduct of IB, and their facilitating effect on the conduct of IB has been, and continues to be, extraordinary.

7.2. The origins of the GATT

In the conduct and study of international business, it is impossible to understand the IB environment unless we understand the WTO—and we cannot begin to understand the WTO unless we understand the historical origins and key provisions of the GATT.

The factors that led to the creation of the GATT can be found in the international trade conditions that developed during the Great Depression (which began in 1930) and in the new political, security, and economic order that was created at the end of the Second World War (WWII).

7.2.1 International trade and the Great Depression

The start of the Great Depression is generally attributed to structural weaknesses in the US economy, which resulted in the stock market crash of 1929.

A primary reason for the severity and duration of the Great Depression was the escalation in the use of protectionist tariffs in the conduct of international trade.[5]

This escalation began in the US with the adoption of the Tariff Act of 1930 (which is commonly referred to as the Smoot–Hawley Tariff), which increased tariff barriers on more than 20,000 categories of products entering the US. The implementation of the Smoot–Hawley Tariff had two principal effects. First, it reduced the value of imports entering the US by more than 50 percent. Second, it prompted other nation-states to apply retaliatory tariffs to US products, which caused US exports to decline by more than 50 percent.

7.2.1.1 Trade as a zero-sum game

Over the next decade, the increased use of protectionist tariffs became a global phenomenon, because the governments of most nation-states saw international trade as a zero-sum game[6] and imposed high tariff barriers to protect their nation-states' economies.

As with the Smoot–Hawley Tariff, these high tariff barriers prompted other nation-states to retaliate by imposing even higher tariffs, which resulted in the further escalation of tariff barriers.

7.2.1.2 The minus-sum downward spiral

The escalation of tariffs by nation-states in the 1930s, and the zero-sum mind-set that dominated the international commercial environment, led to the creation of a minus-sum game:[7] a downward spiral that resulted in a more than 50 percent decline in international trade.

This decline in international trade further adversely affected the economies of individual nation-states and the global economy, and exacerbated and sustained the depression—which continued until the end of the Second World War.[8]

7.2.2 The new political, security, and economic order

The current concepts, principles, and structures that govern the conduct of international business are part of the global political, security, and economic system that was established at the end of WWII.

7.2.2.1 The United Nations

The political and security elements of the post-WWII system are contained in the Charter of the United Nations. This instrument was drafted and signed by representatives of 50 nation-states that met in San Francisco from April to June 1945, and came into force in October 1945.

The UN Charter created the United Nations organization.[9] The UN Charter also delineates the concepts, principles, and procedures that govern the policies and operations of the UN organization, the 70 intergovernmental organizations that make up the UN System,[10] and the international political and security-related behaviors of UN member states.

7.2.2.2 The World Bank and the IMF

The economic elements of the post-WWII system include the World Bank[11] and the International Monetary Fund. The treaties creating these two entities were finalized and signed at the Bretton Woods Conference[12] in the United States in 1944.

The representatives of the 44 nation-states that attended the Bretton Woods Conference also recommended the creation of a third mechanism that would address international trade and other issues related to the conduct of international commerce.[13]

7.2.2.3 The third mechanism

The creation of the third mechanism followed two parallel tracks or initiatives: (1) the General Agreement on Tariffs and Trade, and (2) the International Trade Organization (ITO).[14]

The purpose of the GATT initiative was to create a narrowly focused agreement that would reduce tariffs and other barriers to trade.

The purpose of the ITO initiative was to create a treaty (called the ITO Charter) that would govern all aspects of international commerce—and would establish a global organizational mechanism.

Work on these two initiatives was interrelated and proceeded in parallel. The nation-states that participated in the GATT initiative also participated in the ITO initiative, and it was intended that the text of the GATT instrument would be included as a chapter of the ITO Charter.[15]

7.2.3 The GATT initiative

The GATT initiative was characterized by a sense of urgency. The Second World War had caused huge loss of life, the destruction of property, and the dislocation and dysfunction of the global economy. Many world leaders believed that the extremely high tariffs that had been created during the 1930s threatened the recovery of the global economy.

In December 1945, at the invitation of the US government, representatives from 15 nation-states began talks related to the creation of a binding agreement for reducing tariffs. In October 1947, in Geneva, the participants in this initiative (which had increased to 23 nation-states) finalized work on the GATT instrument.

The 1947 GATT instrument included tariff reductions on about 45,000 product categories[16] that were estimated to affect about 20 percent of world trade, and included a set of trade-related concepts, principles, and functional mechanisms.

7.2.3.1 The implementation of the GATT instrument

The term *agreement* was used in the title of the GATT to expedite its implementation. If the GATT instrument had been called a treaty, it would have been subject to ratification by the governments of the contracting parties, and to the possibility of protracted time delays that can accompany the ratification process.[17] As an agreement, the GATT instrument needed only definitive signature[18] by the required number of contracting parties—and could enter into force without being ratified.

There was, however, a possibility that implementation could be delayed due to the instrument's acceptance requirements.[19] Article XXVI, Acceptance, Entry into Force and Registration, says that for the GATT instrument to enter into force, it must be accepted by governments that "account for 85 per centum of the total external trade" of the nation-states participating in the process.

7.2.3.2 The Protocol of Provisional Application

To expedite implementation and avoid delays due to the 85 percent requirement, eight of the GATT contracting parties[20] signed a Protocol of Provisional Application of the General Agreement on Tariffs and Trade (PPA) on October 30, 1947, which caused Parts I, II, and III of the GATT "to apply provisionally on and after January 1, 1948."[21]

The PPA was "provisional" because it was intended as a temporary measure to achieve immediate implementation of the key provisions of the GATT—while waiting for the 85 percent requirement to be achieved and/or for the ITO Charter to enter into force.

The PPA was later signed by the other GATT initiative participants and became the acceptance procedure used by all subsequent GATT contracting parties.[22]

7.2.4 The ITO initiative

The ITO initiative was characterized by its scope—which was intended to cover all aspects of international commerce.

In February 1946, in response to proposals by the US and the UK, the United Nations Economic and Social Committee (UNESC) created a sub-committee to do preparatory work on the drafting of a charter for an International Trade Organization, and adopted a resolution that called for a conference to draft and adopt the charter.

7.2.4.1 The ITO Charter

The meetings of the sub-committee were held in London in 1946 and 1947. The drafting of the instrument was completed at the United Nations Conference on Trade and Employment in Havana, which began in November 1947 and ended in March 1948. The ITO Charter was signed by 53 nation-states on April 15, 1948.

Chapter IV of the charter, Commercial Policy, included all of the operative articles from the GATT instrument. The only significant difference between the two texts is that the GATT instrument refers to *contracting parties*, whereas the ITO Charter refers to *Members*.

Chapter VII provided for the establishment of the ITO and detailed the rules and procedures that would govern the structure, systems, and operations of the organization.

The charter also included: Chapter II, Employment and Economic Activity; Chapter III, Economic Development and Reconstruction; Chapter V, Restrictive Business Practices; Chapter VI, Intergovernmental Commodity Agreements; and Chapter VIII, Settlement of Differences.

7.2.4.2 Ratification

Article 103 of the charter required that it be ratified before entering into force.[23] Because the United States had led the ITO initiative, most signatories chose to wait until the ITO Charter had been ratified by the US government before submitting it to their own governments for ratification.

In April 1949, the president of the United States presented the ITO Charter to the US Congress for ratification. It was, however, not voted on by either house of the US Congress, and was never ratified by the United States.[24]

Because the ITO Charter was not ratified by the United States, it was not ratified by the minimum number of other signatories, and it did not enter into force. Because the ITO Charter did not enter into force, the International Trade Organization was never created.

7.3 The GATT instrument and mechanism

As a result of the signing of the PPA, the key provisions of the GATT had entered into effect in January 1948. But the failure of the ITO initiative created logistical problems.

Because it was intended that all of the operative articles from the GATT instrument would be implemented by the ITO, the drafters of the GATT instrument had not included any provision for the establishment of a GATT organizational and administrative mechanism. Because the GATT instrument made no provision for an organization, (1) it provided no legal basis for the establishment of an organization and (2) it did not provide a name for the organization.

These problems were solved by borrowing the Interim Commission for the International Trade Organization (ICITO), which had been established by UNESC in Geneva to serve as the secretariat of the ITO, and by changing the name of the ICITO to the GATT Secretariat.[25] The GATT continued to use this ad hoc solution until the GATT Secretariat was replaced by the WTO in 1995.

Because the GATT instrument made no provision for an organization, signatories to the GATT could not be called "members"—but were referred to as "contracting parties."

From January 1, 1948, until December 31, 1994, the 1947 GATT instrument (as amended and supplemented by related instruments) and the GATT organization facilitated trade among the GATT contracting parties, which, by the end of 1994, included 125 nation-states and three separate customs territories.[26]

7.3.1 The objectives and performance of the GATT

To offset and reverse the minus-sum effects of the escalation in tariff barriers by nation-states during the 1930s, the provisions contained in the GATT instrument were designed as a plus-sum game.[27]

7.3.1.1 Reciprocal and mutually advantageous arrangements

The objectives contained in the preamble to the GATT, and the means for achieving these objectives, were based on a plus-sum belief in mutual benefit.

When stating the objectives of the GATT, the preamble says that relations between nation-states:

> should be conducted with a view to raising standards of living, ensuring full employment and a large and steadily growing volume of real income and effective demand, developing the full use of the resources of the world, and expanding the production and exchange of goods.

The preamble says the means for achieving these objectives would be "by entering into reciprocal and mutually advantageous arrangements" for "the substantial reduction of tariffs and other barriers to trade" and "the elimination of discriminatory treatment in international commerce."

7.3.1.2 The extraordinary success of the GATT

Based on its stated objectives, the performance of the GATT instrument and the GATT organization from 1948 until the end of 1994 was extraordinary. By the end of 1994, tariffs, other barriers to trade, and discriminatory treatment in international commerce were a fraction of the levels they had been in 1947.

This extraordinary success was due primarily to the effectiveness of the functional mechanisms contained in the GATT instrument.[28]

7.3.1.3 The functional mechanisms

The GATT instrument includes two functional mechanisms for reducing tariffs (one periodic and the other continuous), and one functional mechanism for eliminating discriminatory treatment:

1. The periodic mechanism for reducing tariffs is "multilateral trade negotiations." This mechanism is discussed in Section 7.3.2.
2. The continuous mechanism for reducing tariffs is "most-favored nation" (MFN). This mechanism is discussed in Section 7.5.1.
3. The mechanism for eliminating discrimination is "national treatment." This mechanism is discussed in Section 7.5.2.

7.3.2 Multilateral trade negotiations

The periodic functional mechanism for reducing tariffs is called *multilateral trade negotiations*, which are commonly referred to as *trade rounds* or simply *rounds*. This mechanism is contained in Article XXVIII of the GATT.

Between 1948 and the end of 1994, the GATT contracting parties participated in and concluded seven rounds of multilateral trade negotiations. Each round was named after the city or country in which the GATT contracting parties were meeting when the round was initiated, or, in two cases, after a person.

7.3.2.1 The Annecy to Tokyo Rounds

Each round has tended to focus on one or more issue areas. During the Annecy (1949), Torquay (1951), and Geneva (1955–1956) rounds, the contracting parties focused on further reducing tariffs on existing product categories and adding new categories.

In subsequent rounds, the contracting parties continued to reduce tariffs, but also began addressing other issue areas that drove the evolution of the GATT instrument and the GATT organization.

The Dillon Round (1960–1962)[29] addressed issues related to the creation of the European Economic Community (EEC); the Kennedy Round (1964–1967)[30] addressed anti-dumping and rules relating to trade negotiations; and the Tokyo Round (1973–1979) developed rules and procedures relating to anti-dumping, licensing, non-tariff barriers, and the settlement of disputes—and developed "plurilateral agreements" that allowed sub-groups of contracting parties to create selective trading agreements.[31]

7.3.2.2 The Uruguay Round

The Uruguay Round (1986–1994) addressed tariffs on textiles and agriculture, non-tariff barriers, trade in services, intellectual property, and the settlement of disputes. The Uruguay Round resulted in the adoption of about 60 agreements, annexes, decisions, and understandings—which included the GATS, TRIPS,[32] and TRIMs;[33] the Agreement on Rules of Origin;[34] and a General Agreement on Tariffs and Trade (GATT).

To differentiate the 1947 and 1994 GATT instruments, they are referred to as GATT 1947 and GATT 1994. GATT 1994 includes all of the provisions contained in GATT 1947, together with its amendments. References to the GATT that do not specify a year are to GATT 1994 and, therefore, to both instruments. When reading or citing from GATT 1947 as part of GATT 1994, it is necessary to change the term *contracting party* to *member.*[35]

The participants in the Uruguay Round also drafted and adopted the Agreement Establishing the WTO. Because this instrument was signed at the ministerial meeting in Marrakesh, it is commonly referred to as the Marrakesh Agreement (MA).

7.4   The establishment of the WTO

From January 1, 1948, until December 31, 1994, GATT 1947 and related instruments were implemented and administered by the GATT organization.

On January 1, 1995, the Agreement Establishing the WTO, GATT 1994, and the other instruments concluded under the Uruguay Round entered into force.

Article 1 of the Marrakesh Agreement is one line. It says "The World Trade Organization (hereinafter referred to as 'the WTO') is hereby established." The organizational provisions contained in the MA replaced the GATT organization.

The principal differences between the GATT organization and the WTO relate to structure, membership, and scope.

7.4.1   Structure

The Marrakesh Agreement details the terms and conditions governing the establishment of the WTO, and the terms and conditions covering its structure, administration, and operations.

7.4.1.1   The Secretariat

Article VI of the MA says the WTO shall have a "Secretariat," "headed by a Director-General."

On January 1, 1995, the GATT Secretariat, located in Geneva, became the WTO Secretariat; the Director-General of the GATT became the Director-General of the WTO.

7.4.1.2   Deliberative and decision-making bodies

Article XVI of the MA says the "WTO shall be guided by the decisions, procedures and customary practices followed by the contracting parties to GATT 1947 and the bodies established in the framework of GATT 1947."

Article IV of the MA defines a hierarchy of deliberative and decision-making bodies. The highest deliberative and decision-making body of the WTO is the Ministerial Conference, "which shall meet at least once every two years. The

Ministerial Conference" and "shall carry out the functions of the WTO and take actions necessary to this effect."

All members of the WTO are members of the Ministerial Conference. Participation in the Ministerial Conference is by a minister (or secretary) of commerce, trade, finance, foreign affairs, agriculture, or other ministerial-level representative from each WTO member. Article VI says the Ministerial Conference appoints the Director-General of the WTO, and defines "the powers, duties, conditions of service, and term of office of the Director-General."

The second-level deliberative and decision-making bodies, which operate continuously, are the General Council, the Dispute Settlement Body, and the Trade Policy Review Body. All members of the WTO are members of these second-level bodies. The second-level bodies report to the Ministerial Conference.

The third-level bodies include the Council for Trade in Goods (Goods Council), the Council for Trade in Services (Services Council), the Council for Trade-Related Aspects of Intellectual Property Rights (TRIPS Council), and six committees that address specific areas. The fourth level includes numerous committees that report to the second- or third-level bodies or councils.

7.4.1.3 Decision making

Article IX of the MA says the "WTO shall continue the practice of decision-making by consensus followed under GATT 1947."[36] If the members are unable to reach a consensus, in most cases "the matter at issue shall be decided by voting" and "decisions of the Ministerial Conference and the General Council shall be taken by a majority of the votes cast."

The exceptions to the simple majority requirement are: (1) membership decisions, which require a two-thirds majority; (2) the waiver of a member's obligation, which requires a three-fourths majority; and (3) amendments to the MA and other WTO instruments, some of which can require a two-thirds majority, a three-fourths majority, or, in some cases, unanimous approval.

7.4.2 Membership

Article XI of the Marrakesh Agreement provides for GATT 1947 contracting parties to become original members of the WTO by signing and ratifying the instruments concluded under the Uruguay Round. Article XII of the MA provides for the accession of other members.

7.4.2.1 Separate customs territories

The members of many intergovernmental organizations, such as the UN, are referred to as *member states*. The members of the WTO, however, are referred to as *members*. This is because Article XII of the MA provides that membership in the WTO is open to nation-states—and to any "separate customs territory possessing full autonomy in the conduct of its external commercial relations."[37]

As of 2014, the membership of the WTO included four SCTs. The European Union, Hong Kong,[38] and Macao, which had been contracting parties of the GATT, became WTO members in 1995. Taiwan became a WTO member in 2002.[39]

7.4.2.2 Members and observers

As of 2014, the WTO had 160 members and 24 observers.

The "separate customs territory" criterion for WTO membership also applies to WTO observers. With the exception of the Holy See (the Vatican), observers must begin membership negotiations within five years after becoming observers.

The accession of new WTO members, and the terms contained in their accession agreements, require the approval of the Ministerial Conference. Although Article XII of the MA says these approvals require a two-thirds majority vote, to date all accessions have been by consensus.

7.4.3 Scope and functions

Articles II and III of the Marrakesh Agreement define the scope and functions of the WTO, which include all of the functions that were formerly performed by the GATT organization. These articles of the MA say the WTO will:

- Provide the common institutional framework for the conduct of trade relations among WTO members
- Facilitate the implementation, administration and operation, and further the objectives, of the instruments concluded under the Uruguay Round
- Provide the forum for trade negotiations among WTO members
- Provide a framework for the implementation of the results of trade negotiations
- Administer the WTO Dispute Settlement Body[40]
- Administer the WTO Trade Policy Review Mechanism

7.4.3.1 Trade in products

Until January 1, 1995, the scope of the GATT 1947 instrument and the GATT organization was limited to trade in products (which is also referred to as trade in goods). Since GATT 1994 entered into force, the primary focus of the WTO has continued to be on trade in products.

7.4.3.2 Trade in services and intellectual property

An important difference between the GATT organization and the WTO is that the scope of the WTO includes two additional areas: (1) trade in services and (2) trade in intellectual property.

These new areas are covered by provisions contained in the MA and two other Uruguay Round instruments: the General Agreement on Trade in Services (GATS) and the Agreement on Trade-Related Aspects of Intellectual Property Rights (TRIPS).

7.4.3.3 The addition of investment

A second and radical difference between the scope of the GATT organization and the scope of the WTO is that the WTO and its instruments cover both trade and investment.

One of the Uruguay Round instruments, the Agreement on Trade-Related Investment Measures (TRIMs), extends the application of two GATT articles (Article III and Article XI) to cover FDI.

This change was radical because, since its inception, the GATT instrument and the GATT organization had focused solely on the trade half of the trade—investment dichotomy.[41]

This change is discussed further in Sections 7.5.2.2 and 7.6.1.

7.5 The key provisions of the GATT

As discussed in Section 7.3.1.3, the GATT includes three functional mechanisms for achieving its objectives.

The periodic functional mechanism for reducing tariffs, "multilateral trade negotiations," is discussed in Section 7.3.2. Since the establishment of the WTO, this mechanism has been continued with the start of the Doha Round in 2001.[42]

The other two functional mechanisms are MFN and national treatment.

7.5.1 MFN

The continuous functional mechanism for reducing tariffs is contained in Part 1, Article I, of the GATT: General Most-Favoured-Nation Treatment.

7.5.1.1 The origin and meaning of the term

The term *most-favoured nation* is from the Treaty of Amity and Commerce Between the United States and France, 1778. When the treaty was being negotiated, the 13 United States of America were at war with England.[43] Before the war, the tariffs on imports from England into the American colonies were significantly lower than the tariffs on imports from France and other countries.

During the treaty negotiations, France's foreign minister stipulated that in the ports of the United States, the subjects of the king of France "shall pay…no other or greater Duties or Imposts…than those which the Nations most favoured are or shall be obliged to pay."[44] The words "Nations most favoured" were used as a euphemism to avoid using the words Great Britain or England.

7.5.1.2 The MFN clause

The "most-favoured-nation" clause in the GATT says that "with respect to customs duties…any advantage, favour, privilege or immunity granted by any member to any product" from any country must be given immediately and unconditionally to the same or similar products from "the territories of all other members."

The US: Trucks

The tariff on trucks entering the US is 25 percent. If the US government reduced the tariff on trucks entering the US from Japan to 20 percent, then, for this category of product, Japan would be the US's most-favored nation. Because the US is a member of the WTO, and because none of the exceptions discussed in Section 7.5.1.4 currently apply to Japan, the US would be required by the GATT's MFN clause to reduce the tariff rate on trucks from all WTO members to 20 percent.

7.5.1.3 How the MFN requirement works

The MFN process is simple but ingenious. To facilitate the export of their products, nation-states are continually negotiating tariff reductions with other nation states. Because of the MFN clause, the lower tariffs agreed to in these bilateral and multi-lateral negotiations must be extended to all WTO members.

The process is ingenious. The governments of nation-states are motivated by national self-interest to negotiate the reduction of tariffs with other nation-states—because they believe this will produce bilateral plus-sum games. By extending these lower tariffs to all WTO members, the MFN requirement converts these multiple bilateral plus-sum games into a global multilateral plus-sum game—that reduces global tariff levels and reduces global barriers to trade.

7.5.1.4 Exceptions to the MFN requirement

The GATT allows several exceptions to the MFN requirement. These exceptions include historical preferences that were in force at the signing of the GATT (Article I);[45] measures necessary to protect public morals, life, and health (Article XX); security exceptions (Article XXI); frontier traffic with adjacent countries (Article XXIV); and the Generalized System of Preferences for products from less-developed countries (Article XXXVI).

Also, Article XXIV says the MFN requirement does not apply to preferential tariffs[46] between members of regional trade blocs.[47] This exception is discussed in Chapter 8, Sections 8.2.2 and 8.6.

7.5.2 National treatment

The functional mechanism for eliminating "discriminatory treatment in international commerce" is contained in Part 1, Article III, of the GATT: National Treatment on Internal Taxation and Regulation.

The "national treatment" provision of the GATT was intended to facilitate trade by preventing discrimination against imported products after they have entered a nation-state.

7.5.2.1 The national treatment clause

The national treatment clause says that "the products of the territory of any Member imported into the territory of any other Member shall not be subject, directly or indirectly, to internal taxes or other internal charges of any kind in excess of those applied, directly or indirectly, to like domestic products" and that these products will "be accorded treatment no less favorable than that accorded to like products of national origin in respect of all laws, regulations and requirements affecting their internal sale, offering for sale, purchase, transportation, distribution or use."

7.5.2.2 The extended application to investment and companies

The national treatment clause of the GATT refers to trade and to products, but not to investment or to companies. As discussed in Section 7.4.3.3, the Agreement on Trade-Related Investment Measures extended the application of the national treatment clause and other provisions of Article III of the GATT to cover FDI.

The changes contained in the TRIMs agreement have also had the effect of extending the application of the national treatment clause from the treatment of products to the treatment of companies.

7.6 The North–South zero-sum game

The replacement of the GATT organization with the WTO was a plus-sum game[48] that benefited all members and benefited companies engaged in the conduct of IB.

Also, the implementation of the GATS instrument,[49] and extending the WTO's area of domain to include both products and services, has been mutually beneficial.

The implementation of the TRIPS and TRIMs instruments,[50] however, has been more problematic. Some of the provisions contained in these instruments can be seen as a North–South zero-sum game that benefits developed countries at the expense of developing countries.

The North–South zero-sum game is most evident, and is having the greatest effect, in three principal WTO issue areas: investment, intellectual property rights (IPR), and agriculture.

7.6.1 Investment

Leaders from some WTO members, and especially those from developed countries, believe the extraordinary success of the GATT on matters related to international trade should be repeated by extending the WTO's mandate to cover FDI.

The investment issue was first formally addressed in the Agreement on Trade-Related Investment Measures (which is discussed in Sections 7.4.3.3 and 7.5.2.2) and in the Singapore Issues.

7.6.1.1 The Singapore Issues

The first WTO Ministerial Conference was held in Singapore in December 1996. This meeting reviewed the entering into force of the Uruguay Round instruments, the establishment of the WTO, and the first two years or the WTO's operations.

This Ministerial Conference also appointed working groups to develop recommendations on four issue areas: (1) trade and investment, (2) trade and competition policy, (3) transparency in governmental procurement, and (4) trade facilitation. These four areas are referred to as the Singapore Issues.

7.6.1.2 The North

The Singapore Issues were proposed by developed countries. If adopted, these issues would further extend the application of national treatment covered in the TRIMs agreement, and would further extend the WTO's mandate over FDI and over the post-entry barriers to FDI that are discussed in Chapter 5.

7.6.1.3 The South

In 1996, developed countries were the home countries[51] of 92 percent of all FDI.[52] The first three Singapore Issues were seen by leaders from many developing countries as benefiting developed countries and their nationals that are foreign direct investors.

Leaders from some developing countries believed the adoption of the Singapore Issues would violate their country's sovereignty, because it would infringe upon their country's right: (1) to regulate FDI access and to regulate post-entry FDI operations, and (2) to formulate and implement domestic economic development policies and strategies.

And leaders from some developing countries argued against the first three Singapore Issues on the grounds that, by definition, the WTO's mandate is limited to trade and that investment issues should be handled by other intergovernmental mechanisms, such as UNCTAD.[53]

7.6.2 Intellectual property rights

In some cases, the North–South zero-sum game is evident not in the provisions of a WTO instrument, but in the interpretation and enforcement of the instrument.

Developing countries have generally supported the Agreement on Trade-Related Aspects of Intellectual Property Rights, but have serious concerns about its implementation.

Access to medicines

Developing-country governments have complained that overly restrictive enforcement of the TRIPS agreement, which treats medicines as consumer products, has limited their ability to access desperately needed medicines at reasonable prices.

In 2000, after the government of South Africa had adopted new IPR legislation, which followed the flexibility provisions contained in TRIPS, 39 pharmaceutical companies from developed countries took legal action against the government and the legislation.

7.6.2.1 The Doha Declaration

The 2001 Doha Declaration, which was adopted by the 4th Ministerial Conference, covered a range of issues including agriculture, services, and intellectual property—and provided the mandate for the Doha Round of Multilateral Trade Negotiations. A section of the declaration, headed TRIPS Agreement and Public Health, addressed some of the concerns of developing countries by restating the flexibility provisions of the agreement.[54]

Some developing countries have maintained, however, that the overly restrictive interpretation and enforcement has continued, and that some developed countries have insisted on provisions in bilateral and regional agreements that exceed TRIPS requirements.

7.6.2.2 TRIPS plus

These behaviors by developed countries are referred to as the *TRIPS plus enforcement trend* or simply as *TRIPS plus.*

In 2010, a group of developed countries introduced a draft Anti-Counterfeit Trade Agreement (ACTA), which includes more restrictive IPR provisions.

7.6.3 Agriculture

Some of the longest-standing and most serious grievances of developing countries are related to restrictions that limit access of their agricultural products to markets in developed countries.

For the South, agriculture can be a critical economic issue: Agriculture accounts for as much as 80 percent of the GDP of some developing countries—and is frequently their principal category of exports and their principal source of foreign exchange.

For the North, agriculture can be a critical political issue. Agriculture accounts for a small percentage of the GDP of most developed countries, but the voting patterns of farmers make them key political constituencies in the US and Japan, and several European countries.

The governments of these economically developed WTO members use tariff and non-tariff barriers to protect politically sensitive segments of their agriculture industries, use export subsidies to support exports by these segments, and/or provide farmers in these segments with subsidies.

7.6.3.1 Subsidies

The most contentious North–South agriculture issue is domestic agriculture subsidies.[55] The primary purpose of these subsidies is not related to trade—but domestic subsidies can produce indirect or secondary effects that act as barriers to trade or distort free trade.[56]

Agriculture subsidies can act as barriers to trade because they make it possible for farmers to reduce the prices at which they sell their products domestically, which can make it more difficult for imported products to compete with domestically produced products.

Agriculture subsidies can distort free trade because they make it possible for farmers to reduce their production costs, which can make it possible for agriculture products to be exported at artificially low prices.

The governments of some developed countries have defended their use of domestic subsidies on the grounds that: (1) the purpose and intent of these subsidies is not trade related, (2) it is their duty and right to support their citizens, and/or (3) interference in this right is a violation of their sovereignty.

7.6.3.2 The Doha Round

Since its inception in 2001, the Doha Round of Multilateral Trade Negotiations[57] has been dominated by the North–South agriculture issues. Developing countries have demanded that developed countries eliminate the use of domestic agriculture subsidies. The response by developed countries has been varied, and has been the cause of dissent between developed countries.

France and the US: Cotton subsidies

France has criticized the US because (despite repeated adverse rulings by the WTO Dispute Settlement Body) the US continues to pay more than $3 billion a year in domestic subsidies to cotton farmers.[58]

The intractability of the agriculture issues is one reason the Doha Round, which was initially scheduled to finish in 2004, has been so conflicted and protracted.

7.6.4 The Cancun Ministerial Conference

The North–South zero-sum game came to a head at the 5th Ministerial Conference in Cancun, in 2003, over the agenda of what would be discussed at the meeting.

The developed countries wanted the Singapore Issues to be the principal items on the agenda; the developing countries wanted the agenda to focus on "development issues." For example, the developed countries wanted the agenda to focus on increasing access for FDI; the developing countries wanted the agenda to focus on the elimination of domestic agriculture subsidies.

On all of these issues, the North and the South both refused to compromise or cede control—and more than 150 ministers who had come to Cancun were unable to agree on an agenda for the four-day meeting. On the third day, the meeting was adjourned before it began.

7.6.5 The Bali Ministerial Conference

In September 2013, Roberto Carvalho de Azevêdo from Brazil became director-general of the WTO. This was the first time, either at the GATT organization or at the WTO, that a person from a South member country had been appointed to this position.

In December 2013, at the 9th Ministerial Conference in Bali, the members adopted unanimously two ministerial declarations and 14 ministerial decisions,[59] most of which are related to Doha Round issues.[60]

The Bali Conference was the first time since the establishment of the WTO that North and South members had reached consensus on a range of important issues, and the conference is seen as a possible turning point for the WTO.[61]

7.6.6 The Nairobi Ministerial Conference

Since the Bali Ministerial Conference, the Director General has reported significant progress on the implementation of the Bali Package and on other Doha Round issues—and, as of December 2014, there were high expectations for the 10th Ministerial Conference, to be held in December 2015 in Nairobi.[62]

7.7 Other global elements

The dominant global elements of the IB environment are the GATT, other WTO instruments, and the WTO. But the IB environment also includes many other important global instruments and mechanisms.

7.7.1 Other global instruments

Non-WTO global intergovernmental instruments that influence the conduct of IB include:

- United Nations Set of Principles and Rules on Competition
- Convention Establishing the World Intellectual Property Organization
- Convention on the Settlement of Investment Disputes between States and Nationals of Other States (the ICSID Convention)
- Convention establishing a Customs Co-operation Council
- Convention on the Valuation of Goods for Customs Purposes (BDV)
- Customs Convention on the International Transit of Goods (the ITI Convention)

- International Convention on the Simplification and Harmonization of Customs Procedures (the Kyoto Convention[63])
- International Convention on the Harmonized Commodity Description and Coding System (the HS Convention)
- United Nations Convention on Contracts for the International Sale of Goods
- Convention on the Recognition and Enforcement of Foreign Arbitral Awards
- Convention on Stolen or Illegally Exported Cultural Objects
- Convention on International Interests in Mobile Equipment
- Convention on the Service Abroad of Judicial and Extrajudicial Documents in Civil or Commercial Matters
- Convention on the Taking of Evidence Abroad in Civil or Commercial Matters

7.7.1.1 UNCTAD Principles and Rules on Competition

The UN Set of Principles and Rules on Competition was created by the United Nations Conference on Restrictive Business Practices, under the auspices of the United Nations Conference on Trade and Development (UNCTAD), between 1978 and 1980. It was adopted by the General Assembly of the United Nations in 1980, and has since been reviewed every five years. This set of principles and rules influences the policies, laws, regulations, and rules of nation-states relating to competition, which can facilitate the FDI operations of foreign-funded companies.

7.7.1.2 WIPO, ICSID, and WCO

The second and third instruments on the above list were created, respectively, by the World Intellectual Property Organization and the International Center on the Settlement of Investment Disputes.

The fourth instrument on the list was created by the Customs Co-operation Council, which in 1995 became the World Customs Organization (WCO). The next four instruments on the list were created by the WCO.

The last four instruments on the list are discussed in Chapter 9, Section 9.1.4.

7.7.2 Other global mechanisms

Non-WTO global intergovernmental mechanisms that influence the conduct of IB include:

- United Nations Conference on Trade and Development, and its Program on Transnational Corporations
- United Nations International Trade Center
- Organisation for Economic Co-operation and Development (OECD)
- World Intellectual Property Organization

- World Customs Organization
- International Center on the Settlement of Investment Disputes
- United Nations Commission for International Trade and Law (UNCITRAL)
- Hague Conference on Private International Law (HCCH)
- International Institute for the Unification of Private Law (UNIDROIT)

The last four mechanisms on this list are discussed in Chapter 9, Section 9.1.4.

Endnotes

1. The term *global* is discussed in Chapter 6, Section 6.2.2.3.
2. WTO membership is discussed in Section 7.4.2.
3. Press release, Azevêdo: Accessions work.
4. A plus-sum game is a win-win situation, structure, or relationship—and is one of three game theory alternatives. The other game alternatives are zero-sum (win-lose) and minus-sum (lose-lose).
5. Protectionist tariffs are discussed in Chapter 2, Section 2.2.4.1.
6. A zero-sum game is a win-lose situation, structure, or relationship. Game theory alternatives are discussed in Endnote 4.
7. A minus-sum game is a lose-lose situation, structure, or relationship.
8. WWII began in 1937 in Asia and in 1939 in Europe, and ended in 1945.
9. The first meeting of the United Nations organization was held in London in January 1946.
10. UN System, structure, and organization.
11. The World Bank is one of the operating units of the International Bank for Reconstruction and Development (IBRD). The IBRD is commonly referred to as the World Bank.
12. The official name of the Bretton Woods Conference is the United Nations Monetary and Financial Conference.
13. The Bretton Woods Conference did not create this third mechanism, because the conference was attended primarily by ministers of finance, and not by ministers of trade and/or commerce.
14. The ITO initiative is discussed in Section 7.2.4.
15. Chapter IV of the ITO Charter is discussed in Section 7.2.4.1.
16. Product categories are discussed in Chapter 2, Section 2.2.2.
17. The ratification process is discussed in Chapter 6, Section 6.3.3.1.
18. The term *definitive signature* is discussed in Chapter 6, Section 6.3.3.3.
19. Acceptance procedures are discussed in Chapter 6, Section 6.3.3.
20. The initial signatories to the PPA were Australia, Belgium, Canada, France, Luxemburg, the Netherlands, the UK, and the US.
21. The PPA provided that Part I and Part III of the GATT (Articles I and II, and XXIV to XXXV) be applied, and that Part II (Articles III to XXIII) be applied "to the fullest extent not inconsistent with existing legislation." The PPA did not cover Part IV, Trade and Development.
22. In practice, the PPA replaced Article XXVI as the GATT's acceptance procedure.
23. As discussed in Chapter 6, Sections 6.3.2 and 6.3.3, a charter is a type of treaty, and treaties must be ratified by a minimum number of signatory states before entering into force.
24. The U.S. House Committee on Foreign Affairs held hearings on the ITO Charter, but it was never voted on by the committee and was not submitted to the House of Representatives for their consideration.

25. This name caused some confusion, because it was unclear if a reference to the GATT was to the GATT instrument or to the GATT organization. From 1948 until 1965, the GATT Secretariat was headed by an Executive Secretary; from 1965 until December 31, 1994, it was headed by a Director-General.
26. The terms *nation-state* and *separate customs territory* are discussed in Chapter 6, Section 6.1.
27. Game theory alternatives are discussed in Endnote 4.
28. Functional mechanisms are discussed in Chapter 6, Section 6.4.2.
29. The Dillon Round was named after US Treasury Secretary Douglas Dillon, who proposed the round.
30. The Kennedy Round was named in honor of the 35th President of the United States, John F. Kennedy, who had been assassinated in 1963.
31. The creation of new plurilateral agreements was discontinued following the establishment of the WTO.
32. GATS and TRIPS are discussed in Sections 7.4.3.2 and 7.6.
33. TRIMs is discussed in Sections 7.4.3.3, 7.5.2.2, 7.6, and 7.6.1.2.
34. The Agreement on Rules of Origin is discussed in Chapter 2, Sections 2.2.3.2 and 2.2.3.3.
35. GATT 1994, Article 2(a), says that "references to 'contracting party' in the provisions of GATT 1994 shall be deemed to read 'Member.'"
36. Article XXV of GATT 1947 says that, with some exceptions, decisions "shall be approved by a two-thirds majority of the votes cast and that such majority shall comprise more than half of the contracting parties." In practice, however, decisions were adopted by consensus. This meant a decision could be blocked by a single dissenting contracting party.
37. The use and definition of the term *separate customs territory* in Article XII of the MA were borrowed from Article XXXIII of GATT 1947. The term *separate customs territory* is discussed in Chapter 6, Section 6.1.1.3.
38. Hong Kong is listed by the WTO as Hong Kong, China.
39. Taiwan joined under the name Separate Customs Territory of Taiwan, Penghu, Kinmen, and Matsu (Chinese Taipei) and is listed by the WTO as Chinese Taipei.
40. The WTO Dispute Settlement Body is discussed in Chapter 9, Section 9.5.
41. The trade–investment dichotomy is discussed in Chapter 2, Section 2.1.
42. The Doha Round is discussed in Section 7.6.3.2.
43. This war is discussed in Chapter 8, Section 8.5.1.3.
44. Treaty of Amity and Commerce, Article 3.d. Article 4 of the treaty provides these same trade privileges to the "Subjects, People and Inhabitants of the said United States" in ports controlled by France—and also includes the words "Nations most favoured."
45. Preferences are discussed in Chapter 8, Section 8.2.1.2.
46. Preferential tariffs are discussed in Chapter 8, Sections 8.3.1.1 and 8.3.1.7.
47. Regional trade blocs are discussed in Chapter 8, Section 8.2.
48. Game theory alternatives are discussed in Endnote 4.
49. The GATS instrument is discussed in Section 7.4.3.2.
50. The TRIPS and TRIMS instruments are discussed in Sections 7.4.3.2 and 7.4.3.3.
51. The term *home country* is discussed in Chapter 6, Section 6.1.1.2.
52. Foreign direct investment is discussed in Chapter 4, Section 4.1.
53. UNCTAD is discussed in Section 7.1.1.
54. Doha Declaration, 17–19.
55. Subsides are defined and discussed in Chapter 3, Section 3.2.
56. The distortion of free trade is discussed in Chapter 3, Section 3.2.2.

57. The Doha Round is also called the Doha Development Round, or the Doha Development Agenda, because this round was intended to address the needs of developing countries.
58. US cotton subsidies are discussed in Chapter 3, Section 3.2.4.3.
59. To achieve this result, the conference was extended from four to five days, and the last days of the conference included round-the-clock negotiations.
60. The WTO Bali Ministerial Declaration and Decisions are referred to as the Bali Package.
61. Press release, Consultations produce Bali Package.
62. Press release, Let's make sure 2015.
63. This instrument is distinct from the Kyoto Protocol (the United Nations Framework Convention on Climate Change).

8 Regional and bilateral instruments and mechanisms

Contents

8.1 Regional integration agreements

When nation-states from the same geographical region cooperate for the purpose of achieving economic, political, security-related, social, cultural, and other mutually beneficial goals, this is referred to as *regional integration.*

The instruments nation-states negotiate, enter into, implement, and administer to effect regional integration are referred to as *regional integration agreements* (RIAs).

ASEAN

In 1967, Indonesia, Malaysia, Philippines, Singapore, and Thailand signed an instrument called The ASEAN Declaration, which created the Association of Southeast Asian Nations. The preamble to the declaration states that ASEAN was being created to "accelerate the economic growth, social progress and cultural development in the region" and to "promote regional peace and stability."

The GCC

In 1981, Bahrain, Kuwait, Oman, Qatar, Saudi Arabia, and the United Arab Emirates created the Cooperation Council for the Arab States of the Gulf, which is commonly referred to as the Gulf Cooperation Council, "to effect coordination, integration and inter-connection between Member States in all fields in order to achieve unity between them."[1]

The initialism RIA can have three meanings. It can refer to: (1) a *regional integration agreement*; (2) a *regional integration area*, which is the geographical area covered by the nation-states that are participants in a regional integration agreement; and/or (3) the organizational mechanism that is created to implement and administer a regional integration agreement.

There are hundreds of RIAs, which include:

- African Union (AU)
- Andean Community (Pacto Andino)
- Commonwealth of Independent States (CIS)
- European Union
- Gulf Cooperation Council (GCC)
- North American Free Trade Area (NAFTA)
- North Atlantic Treaty Organization (NATO)
- Shanghai Cooperation Organization (SCO)

- South Asian Association for Regional Cooperation (SAARC)
- West African Economic and Monetary Union (WAEMU)

8.1.1 Levels of regional integration

The degree to which an RIA is integrated is referred to as its *level of integration*. Levels of integration are related directly to the extent to which an RIA's member states surrender parts of their sovereignty.[2]

When referring to an RIA's level of integration, the terms *limited integration* and *deep integration* define the ends of a continuum.

ASEAN

When ASEAN was created, it was near the limited-integration end of the continuum. The ASEAN Declaration, which created the organization, refers to "the will of the member nations…to bind themselves together in friendship and cooperation and, through joint efforts and sacrifices."

ASEAN's founding member nations chose this language to create an organization that would give them the benefits of a closer relationship, but would not require them to give up significant parts of their sovereignty.

The EU

The European Union is near the deep-integration end of the continuum. In 1957, Belgium, France, West Germany, Italy, Luxembourg, and the Netherlands entered into the Treaty of Rome,[3] which created the European Economic Community—and provided for the progressive reduction in tariff and non-tariff barriers, and for reducing restrictions on the movement of products, people, and capital between EEC member states.

In 1992, the 12 members of the EEC entered into the Maastricht Treaty,[4] which created the European Union. The Maastricht Treaty and its several amendments have deepened the EU's level of integration by requiring member states to incrementally give up or surrender additional parts of their sovereignty, including those parts related to international trade policy and the regulation of international trade.

As of 2014, the EU had 28 member states[5] and includes shared political, juridical, and banking institutions; shared foreign policy and military policy; shared legal systems and laws, regulations, and product standards; a monetary union;[6] and the right of its citizens to live and work in any member country.

8.1.2 Changes in levels of integration and operational areas

Although the evolution of the EU is exceptional, it is not unusual for RIAs to evolve. RIAs frequently increase their number of member states and/or increase their levels of integration. Also, it is not unusual for RIAs to change and/or expand their operational areas of domain.

ASEAN

ASEAN, which now has ten members,[7] is evolving and becoming a more deeply integrated RIA. ASEAN Vision 2020 (which was adopted at ASEAN's annual meeting in 1997) and the ASEAN Charter (which was signed in Singapore in 2008) include provisions that, when implemented, will increase significantly ASEAN's level of integration.

The ASEAN Charter also expanded ASEAN's area of domain. For example, Article 14 of the charter says "ASEAN shall establish an ASEAN human rights body."

The SCO

In 1996, the leaders of China and four former members of the Soviet Union—Russia, Kazakhstan, Kyrgyzstan, and Tajikistan—met in Shanghai and created the Shanghai Five Mechanism, which was an ad hoc functional mechanism for resolving border disputes between China and each of the other members.

At the 2001 meeting in Shanghai, Uzbekistan was added as the sixth member, and the members created the Shanghai Cooperation Organization. At the 2002 meeting in St. Petersburg, the members adopted the SCO Charter. In 2004, the SCO Secretariat was established in Beijing.[8]

Following the resolution of all border disputes between China and the other members, the focus of the SCO shifted to security-related issues and joint military exercises, and has been extended to include economic development, international trade, and foreign investment.

8.1.3 The comparative advantages of RIAs

There are several reasons nation-states choose to establish and use RIAs—rather than global instruments and mechanisms—to achieve economic, political, security-related, and other goals. These reasons include focus, size, compatibility, and operational effectiveness.

8.1.3.1 Geographical proximity and focus

A primary factor that drives the creation of regional intergovernmental organizations is their geographical proximity and their regional or sub-regional focus.

In some cases, regional organizations (such as the EU, the AU, the CIS, and the GCC) address a wide range of political, economic, and security-related areas. But all RIAs focus on operational issues that are of specific importance to their geographical region or sub-region.

The GCC

The founding members of the GCC are all located in the Persian Gulf sub-region of the Middle East; they share common borders; and they "adopt common stands" on "issues that are of common concern."[9]

8.1.3.2 Size

The focus advantage of RIAs is made possible by their relatively small size. As of 2014, the UN had 193 member states and the WTO had 160 members. RIAs, however, have far fewer members.

The EU has 28 members, the CIS has 11, ASEAN has 10, the SCO and the GCC each has 6, and NAFTA has 3. The largest RIA is the AU, which has 54 members.[10]

8.1.3.3 Compatibility

A further advantage of the geographical proximity, focus, and smaller size of RIAs is that these factors can reduce the range of their members' political, social, cultural, or economic-development differences.

The GCC

In addition to their geographical proximity and shared focus, members of the GCC share similar levels of economic development, share the same language, share "common qualities and similar systems founded on the creed of Islam,"[11] and are all Arab oil-producing states.

The AU

There is a high degree of ethnic, cultural, religious, and language diversity among the 54 member states of the African Union. But they are all developing countries, and within the AU they do not have to contend with being bullied by more powerful and developed nation-states.

8.1.3.4 Operational effectiveness

The geographical proximity, focus, smaller size, and relative compatibility of RIAs facilitate better communication between their member states; can make it less difficult for member states to achieve agreement on key issues; can make it possible to find solutions that are acceptable to all member states; and can improve the implementation and effectiveness of decisions.

8.1.4 Types of RIAs

RIAs can be grouped into three primary classifications: economic, political, and security-related. The forced application these classifications can, however, be misleading—because economic, political, and security-related issues are often highly interdependent and many RIAs cover two or all three classifications.

The GCC

The GCC says its functional areas include "economic cooperation; cooperation in the field of human and environment affairs; security cooperation, military cooperation, media cooperation, and legal and judicial cooperation; cooperation in the field of political affairs; and cooperation in the field of auditing."[12]

Each of these functional areas includes sub-categories. For example, the field of human and environment affairs includes "cooperation in education, scientific and technical cooperation, cooperation in the field of human resources, joint social action, joint cultural action, environmental cooperation, cooperation in the field of health, joint municipal action, joint action in the field of housing, joint youth action, [and] joint sport action."

8.2 Regional trade blocs

If the purpose of an RIA is to effect economic integration and to create mutual economic benefit by reducing or eliminating barriers to trade, it is referred to as a *regional trade bloc* or *regional trading bloc* (RTB).

More than one-third of the world's trade occurs within RTBs.

The ASEAN FTA

In 1992, the members of ASEAN extended the scope of their RIA by creating an RTB called the ASEAN Free Trade Area. The purpose of this new mechanism was to "promote greater economic efficiency, productivity, and competitiveness" by "eliminating tariff and non-tariff barriers among the member countries."

NAFTA

In 1993, Canada, Mexico, and the US entered into the North American Free Trade Agreement,[13] which, on January 1, 1994,[14] created an RTB called the North American Free Trade Area.

Article 102 of NAFTA lists six objectives: eliminate barriers to trade, promote fair competition, increase investment opportunities, protect intellectual property rights, create procedures for the implementation and administration of the agreement and for the resolution of disputes, and establish a framework for further cooperation.

Although the term *regional trade bloc* refers specifically to trade, most RTBs also facilitate FDI between their member states.

The WTO refers to RTBs as *regional trade agreements* (RTAs). As of 2014, there were about 550 RTAs registered with the WTO—of which about 350 had entered into force.

RTBs include:

- ASEAN Free Trade Area (ASEAN FTA)
- Caribbean Community and Common Market (CARICOM)
- Central American Common Market (CACM)
- China–ASEAN Free Trade Area
- Common Market for Eastern and Southern Africa

- Economic Community of West African States (ECOWAS)
- Economic and Monetary Community of Central Africa
- European Union
- Gulf Cooperation Council (GCC)
- Indian Ocean Commission
- Latin America and Andean Pact (Pacto Andino)
- Latin American Integration Association (LAIA)
- North American Free Trade Area
- South Asian Association for Regional Cooperation
- Southern African Development Community (SADC)
- Southern Cone Common Market (MERCOSUR)
- Sub-Saharan Africa Cross-Border Initiative
- West African Economic and Monetary Union

8.2.1 The effects and characteristics of RTBs

RTBs facilitate regional economic integration, and create mutual economic benefit for member states, by:

- Reducing or eliminating tariff and non-tariff barriers
- Reducing entry and post-entry barriers to FDI
- Providing the regulatory and operational parameters that govern or influence the conduct of trade and FDI between the member states
- Providing mechanisms for the harmonization of laws that affect the conduct of IB, and for the settlement of IB-related disputes[15]

8.2.1.1 Free trade organizations

If the stated purpose of an RTB is to reduce trade barriers to zero, it is called a *free trade organization*.

The term *free trade organization* does not mean there are no trade barriers between the member states of the organization. Rather, it means the goal of the organization is to reduce trade barriers (including tariff barriers and non-tariff barriers) to zero.

8.2.1.2 Preferences and PTAs

When an importing country reduces the customs tariff on a product category from an exporting country, this is referred to as providing the exporting country with a *preference*.

The terms *preference*, *preferential*, *preferential treatment*, *preferential arrangements*, and *preferential rate* are widely used in the conduct of international commerce. For example, these terms appear 54 times in the GATT.

Because the primary mechanism for reducing or eliminating trade barriers within RTBs is the granting of trade preferences, some RTBs are referred to as *preferential trade areas* (PTAs).[16]

8.2.2 RTBs and MFN

A key provision of the GATT is the most-favored nation requirement,[17] which provides that "with respect to customs duties…any advantage, favor, privilege or immunity" granted to any WTO member must be granted to all WTO members.

Article XXIV of the GATT provides, however, that when the members of an RTB reduce tariff levels on trade within their RTB, they are not required to grant these preferences to other WTO members.[18] This exception applies to all RTBs that are registered with the WTO, including bilateral RTBs.[19]

NAFTA

Following the implementation of the tariff phase-out provisions contained in the North American Free Trade Agreement, "the US simple average tariff applied to imports from Mexico declined from 4.01 percent in 1989…to 0.52 percent in 2001."[20] The US was not required to extend these tariff reductions to all WTO members, because these preferences are between members of an RTB that is registered with the WTO.

8.2.3 Free trade areas and customs unions

The two principal types of RTBs are free trade areas (FTAs) and customs unions (CUs).[21] The purpose of both FTAs and CUs is to reduce or eliminate trade barriers between their member states.

The differences between FTAs and CUs are structural and operational. The structural difference is that FTAs and CUs have significantly different levels of integration.[22] The operational difference relates to the setting of external trade policy and to the setting of external tariffs and NTBs.

8.3 Free Trade Areas

FTAs are relatively limited integration RIAs: They require their member states to surrender relatively small amounts of their trade-related sovereignty.

The initialism FTA, like the initialism RIA, can be ambiguous: It can refer to a free trade agreement and/or to a free trade area.

As with the term *free trade organization*, the term *free trade area* does not mean there are no barriers to trade within the FTA. The term means that the purpose and intent of the FTA is to progressively reduce and eventually eliminate intramural barriers to trade.

FTAs, and their number of members as of 2014, include:

- ASEAN Free Trade Area (10 members)
- Central European Free Trade Area (7 members)
- China–ASEAN Free Trade Area (11 members)
- Greater Arab Free Trade Area (16 members)
- North American Free Trade Area (3 members)
- South Asia Free Trade Area (7 members)

8.3.1 Trade policies and tariffs

In FTAs, there is an important distinction between the regulation of internal and external trade policies and tariffs.

8.3.1.1 Internal trade policies and tariffs

An FTA's internal trade policies and customs tariff rates are common. FTA member states have transferred to the FTA their sovereign authority to set trade policies and customs tariffs that govern trade within their FTA. This principle also applies to the use of NTBs within FTAs.

In FTAs, the common internal tariffs are referred to as *preferential tariffs*. In most FTAs, the preferential tariffs are extremely low or zero.

The ASEAN FTA: Shoes within the FTA

Within the ASEAN FTA, the tariff on shoes is zero—if their country of origin is an ASEAN FTA member state.

8.3.1.2 External trade policies and tariffs

An FTA's external trade policies and customs tariff rates are not common. Each FTA member state has retained its sovereign authority to set trade policy and set tariffs with nation-states that are not members of the FTA. This principle also applies to the external use of NTBs.

The ASEAN FTA: External tariffs on shoes

The tariff on shoes entering Thailand from outside the ASEAN FTA is 30 percent. The tariff on shoes entering Singapore from outside the FTA is zero.

The China–ASEAN FTA

Because an FTA's external trade policies and tariff rates are not common, when China was negotiating the China–ASEAN Free Trade Area, it was necessary for China to negotiate a separate agreement with each ASEAN member state.

8.3.1.3 The effect of the absence of common external tariffs

The absence of common external trade policies and tariffs can be problematic when a product from outside an FTA enters through a member state that has a low external tariff, and is then transshipped to a member state that has a higher external tariff.

The ASEAN FTA: The transshipment of shoes

A manufacturer from outside the ASEAN FTA could try to avoid paying Thailand's 30 percent tariff on shoes—by importing shoes into Singapore (paying zero tariff) and then transshipping the shoes to Thailand.

8.3.1.4 Rules of origin

To control this problem, FTAs establish and implement rules of origin. As discussed in Chapter 2, Section 2.2.3.1, ROO are divided into two distinct categories: preferential and non-preferential.

Some aspects of preferential and non-preferential rules of origin are the same. The purpose of both categories is to provide criteria that can be used to determine a product's country of origin. In both cases, the term *country of origin* does not refer to the nation-state from where a product was exported, but refers to the nation-state where a product was produced or manufactured. Also, the substantial transformation criterion,[23] which is used when determining non-preferential country of origin, is used in most FTAs.

8.3.1.5 Preferential rules of origin

The principal differences between the two ROO categories are that preferential ROO:

1. Apply to trade between members of an FTA
2. Are not covered by the Kyoto Convention or the Agreement on Rules of Origin[24]
3. Are set and enforced by the members of each FTA
4. Often use a more complex set of criteria than non-preferential ROO
5. Frequently include criteria relating to the country of origin of the materials and components used in a product's production or manufacture

8.3.1.6 Substantial transformation

The three methods for determining substantial transformation that are discussed in Chapter 2, Section 2.2.3.3, are also used by FTAs when determining country of origin. Some FTAs modify one of the three methods or combine elements from different methods.

The ASEAN FTA: The value-added method

When determining what constitutes a substantial transformation, the ROO for the ASEAN FTA use the value-added method.[25]

A product is eligible for ASEAN preferential treatment if "the total value of the materials, parts or produce originating from non-ASEAN countries or of undetermined origin used does not exceed 60% of the FOB value of the product produced or obtained and the final process of the manufacture is performed within the territory of the exporting Member State" or if "the aggregate ASEAN content of the final product is not less than 40%."[26]

NAFTA: The change-in-tariff-classification method

The NAFTA Rules of Origin are contained in Chapter 4 of the North American Free Trade Agreement. The NAFTA ROO[27] are based on the HS codes[28] contained in the Harmonized Tariff Schedule of the US Annotated (HTSUSA),[29] and use the change-in-tariff-classification method[30] (which is also called the *tariff-shift method*) when determining substantial transformation.

In the NAFTA ROO, however, the change-in-tariff-classification method is combined with product-specific local content criteria. For example, when cotton fibers, HTSUSA 5201, are spun into cotton yarn, the HS code changes to HTSUSA 5205. But, if the cotton fibers are imported from a non-NAFTA country into Mexico, and spun into cotton yarn in Mexico, the change in HS code does not satisfy NAFTA's substantial transformation requirement—and a US importer of the yarn may not claim that Mexico is the country of origin. Even if the cotton fibers are from Mexico, but the yarn includes more than 7 percent polyester staple fiber from a non-NAFTA country, the yarn (5205.13) would "not originate" in Mexico.[31]

In some cases, the NAFTA ROO combine the change-in-tariff-classification method with the value-added method, which in NAFTA ROO is called *regional value content*.

8.3.1.7 Transshipments within an FTA

An FTA's preferential tariffs apply only to products originating within the FTA. If products that do not comply with an FTA's ROO are transshipped within the FTA, they are subject to tariffs as if they were being imported from outside the FTA.

The ASEAN FTA: The transshipment of shoes

If shoes from outside the ASEAN FTA enter Singapore at no tariff and are transshipped to Thailand, they will be subject to 30 percent tariff when entering Thailand.

In some cases, the administration and enforcement of ROO is made more complex and difficult because of the use of false labeling.

8.3.2 Logistical support

FTAs can be either functional mechanisms or organizational mechanisms.[32] FTAs that are closer to the limited-integration end of the continuum are more likely to be functional mechanisms. FTAs that are closer to the deep-integration end of the continuum,[33] or are moving toward the deep-integration end of the continuum, are more likely to be organizational mechanisms.

NAFTA

The NAFTA is a limited-integration RIA and is primarily a functional mechanism. One of the objectives listed in Article 102 of the agreement is to "create effective procedures for the implementation and application of this Agreement, for its joint administration and for the resolution of disputes." This objective says nothing about creating an organization to implement and administer the agreement.

Most of NAFTA's logistical support is provided by departments or agencies of the governments of Canada, Mexico, and the United States. NAFTA's only separate organizational component is the three secretariat sections (one in the national capital of each member state) that are responsible for the dispute settlement provisions of the agreement.[34]

The ASEAN FTA

The ASEAN FTA began as a limited-integration RIA, but has been moving toward the deep-integration end of the continuum. This FTA is an organizational mechanism: It is part of the ASEAN organization that has a secretariat, a secretary general, an administrative and operational structure, officers, employees, and physical facilities—which are located in Jakarta.[35]

8.4 Customs Unions

CUs are relatively deep-integration RIAs: They require their member states to surrender most or all of their trade-related sovereignty.

CUs include:

- Andean Community (CAN)
- Customs Union of Belarus, Kazakhstan, and Russia
- East Africa Community (EAC)
- European Union
- Gulf Cooperation Council (GCC)
- Southern African Customs Union (SACU)
- Southern Common Market

Several RIAs are working toward becoming customs unions. These prospective CUs include: the African Economic Community, the Arab Customs Union, the Central American Common Market, the Economic Community of West African States, and the Union of South American Nations.

8.4.1 Trade policies and tariffs

Like FTAs, CUs have common internal policies and tariffs.

Unlike FTAs, CUs have common external trade policies, common external tariff rates, and common external NTBs. When a nation-state becomes a member of a CU, it transfers to the CU its sovereign authority to regulate international trade.

GCC

In 2003, the GCC FTA became a CU. The GCC's Supreme Council abolished all "customs duties...regulations and procedures restricting trade among the member States" and implemented "unified customs duties…and trade and customs regulations for trade with non-member States."[36]

Because CU members have transferred to the CU their trade-related regulatory authority, they no longer have the authority to set their own tariff rates, create and apply their own NTBs, or enter into bilateral or multilateral trade agreements.

The EU

The European Union is a customs union. The 28 member states of the EU have transferred their sovereign authority over internal and external trade-related issues to the EU. The EU sets the tariff rates (and governs the use of non-tariff barriers) on all products entering and leaving the EU, and the EU represents its member states in trade negotiations with other nation-states.

The EU and Canada

The Canada–EU Comprehensive Economic and Trade Agreement[37] is a bilateral FTA between Canada and the EU.[38] Because the EU is a customs union, the tariff levels and other terms and conditions contained in CETA apply to all EU member states.

Because CUs have common internal and external trade policies and tariffs, a CU can be referred to as a *common market* or a *single market*.

8.4.1.1 Country of origin

The country of origin issue, which is problematic for transshipments within FTAs, does not exist in CUs. Because CUs have common internal and external trade policies and tariffs, all member states apply the same tariff to a product category entering their CU. Once a product has entered the CU, it is treated the same as products that are produced or manufactured within the CU.

The EU: The transshipment of shoes

The tariff on shoes from outside the EU entering the UK, France, Spain, Italy, or any other EU member state is 8 percent. Once shoes from outside the FTA have entered the EU, and have paid the common EU tariff, they can be transshipped to any other EU member state without paying any additional customs duties.

8.4.1.2 Levels of integration

Compared to FTAs, all CUs are deep-integration RIAs, but not all CUs have the same level of integration. External trade policies and trade-related regulations are less unified in some CUs,[39] and in some CUs different member states have different external trade quotas.

8.4.1.3 Logistical support

Because all CUs are deep-integration RIAs, all CUs are organizational mechanisms. CUs that have deeper levels of integration, and more unified trade policies and trade-related regulations, tend to have more established and more extensive organizational mechanisms. For example, the EU is the most deeply integrated CU—and has the most fully developed CU organizational mechanism.[40]

8.4.2 The surrender of trade-related sovereignty

CUs have the advantage of avoiding the country-of-origin problems that are associated with transshipments within FTAs, but this advantage comes at a price. The member states of CUs have given up their sovereign authority to set trade policy and set tariffs, and to make individual decisions and take individual actions related to the protection of their country's products, companies, industries, and jobs.

Italy, Spain, France, and Germany: Shoes, prices, and protection

The EU has set a low tariff on shoes, which benefits the nationals of member states by avoiding adding significantly to the price of imported shoes. But the low tariff has an adverse effect on leather and shoe industry manufacturers, suppliers, and employees in the EU—and especially on those in the large leather and shoe industries in Italy, Spain, France, and Germany.

Because the governments of Italy, Spain, France, and Germany (and other EU countries) have given up their trade-related sovereignty, they are no longer able to apply country-specific tariffs or NTBs to protect their nationals in their leather and shoe industries.

8.4.3 CUs and separate customs territories

Article XII of the MA defines a separate customs territory as an entity "possessing full autonomy in the conduct of its external commercial relations."[41]

Because CUs have common external trade policies, common external tariffs, and common external NTBs, they are seen as complying with the definition of a separate customs territory.

The European Union was accepted as a member of the WTO in 1995. In the future, other CUs could become members of the WTO.[42]

8.5 Bilateral agreements

In the conduct of IR, the term *bilateral* indicates participation by two nation-states. In the conduct of international commercial relations, the term also applies to participation by a nation-state and a separate customs territory or by two separate customs territories.

8.5.1 Bilateral instruments

As with RIAs, bilateral instruments between nation-states can be commercial, political, or security-related. Most bilateral international agreements, however, are commercial.

In the conduct of international commerce, the factor that distinguishes the role of bilateral instruments from global and regional instruments is specificity.

8.5.1.1 Compared to global instruments

The GATT and other WTO instruments provide the legal and operational framework of the IB environment, and prescribe the concepts, principles, rules, and requirements that govern the conduct of IB.

Bilateral instruments, on the other hand, facilitate the conduct of IB by specifying the terms and conditions that govern trade and FDI between two nation-states, and by reducing or removing specific bilateral barriers to trade and investment.

8.5.1.2 Compared to regional instruments

The specificity of bilateral instruments also differentiates them from RIAs. RIAs frequently cover a combination of commercial, political, and security-related areas— whereas most bilateral instruments focus solely on one of these operational areas.

Even when two nation-states negotiate an agreement that covers two or all three areas, the commercial, political, and security-related elements of the agreement are usually contained in separate instruments.

8.5.1.3 The interdependence of commercial, security, and political treaties

When nation-states negotiate commercial, political, and security-related instruments at the same time, it is not unusual for the acceptance of each instrument to be conditioned on the acceptance of the other instrument or instruments.

The US: Treaties

Beginning in 1776, the US wanted France as an ally in its War of Independence with England. France was England's traditional enemy, but would not agree to enter the war in support of the US unless it had a defense treaty with the US— and France would not agree to a defense treaty with the US unless the US first agreed to sign a Treaty of Amity and Commerce.[43]

8.5.2 Bilateral mechanisms

Bilateral instruments create bilateral functional mechanisms.[44] The logistical support for the implementation, administration, and operations of these functional mechanisms is provided by the government departments of the nation-states that are parties to the instruments.

8.6 Bilateral RTBs

Article XXIV of the GATT says the MFN requirement contained in Article I of the GATT does not apply to preferences between members of a regional trade bloc.[45]

This exception to the MFN requirement applies to all RTBs that are registered with the WTO, even if the RTB has only two members.

The US: Bilateral RTBs

The United States is a member of 12 bilateral RTBs (which include nine bilateral FTAs and three bilateral TPAs[46]): the US–Israel FTA (1985), the US–Chile FTA (2004), the US–Singapore FTA (2004), the US–Australia FTA (2005), the US–Morocco FTA (2006), the US–Peru TPA (2006), the US–Bahrain FTA (2006), the US–Colombia TPA (2006), the US–Panama TPA (2007), the US–Oman FTA (2009), the US–Jordan FTA (2010), and the US–Republic of Korea FTA (2012).

Bilateral RTBs can include two nation-states, a nation-state and a separate customs territory (such as the Canada–EU Comprehensive Economic and Trade Agreement, and the China–Hong Kong Mainland and Hong Kong Closer Economic Partnership Arrangement), or two separate customs territories.

Endnotes

1. GCC Charter, Article 4.
2. The partial surrender of sovereignty is discussed in Chapter 6, Section 6.1.2.4.
3. The official name of the Treaty of Rome is the Treaty Establishing the European Economic Community. The treaty entered into force in 1958.
4. The official name of the Maastricht Treaty is the Treaty on European Union. The treaty entered into force in 1993.
5. As of 2014, the EU member states were: Austria, Belgium, Bulgaria, Croatia, Cyprus, the Czech Republic, Denmark, Estonia, Finland, France, Germany, Greece, Hungary, Ireland, Italy, Latvia, Lithuania, Luxembourg, Malta, the Netherlands, Poland, Portugal, Romania, Slovakia, Slovenia, Spain, Sweden, and the UK.
6. Not all EU member states are members of the European Monetary Union. Monetary unions are discussed in Chapter 10, Section 10.1.1.2.
7. As of 2014, the ASEAN member states were: Brunei, Cambodia, Indonesia, Laos, Malaysia, Myanmar, Philippines, Singapore, Thailand, and Vietnam.
8. As of 2014, the SCO had five observer states: India, Iran, Mongolia, Pakistan, and Turkmenistan.
9. GCC, Most Important Objectives. The "Persian Gulf" and "shared common borders" characteristics of GCC members could change, because, as of 2014, Jordan, Morocco, and Yemen were in the process of becoming members.
10. The AU includes all African nation-states except Morocco.
11. GCC, Foundations and Objectives.
12. GCC, Areas of Cooperation Achievements.
13. This agreement superseded the 1987 Canada–US Free Trade Agreement (CUSFTA).
14. The signing and ratification of NAFTA is discussed in Chapter 6, Section 6.3.3.1.

15. The harmonization of laws and the settlement of disputes are discussed in Chapter 9.
16. See Endnote 21.
17. The most-favored nation provision of the GATT is discussed in Chapter 7, Section 7.5.1.
18. Exceptions to the MFN requirement are discussed in Chapter 7, Section 7.5.1.4.
19. Bilateral RTBs are discussed in Section 8.6.
20. Agama and McDaniel, "NAFTA and US–Mexico Trade."
21. A third RTB category is preferential trade areas (PTAs), which have a lower level of integration than FTAs. PTAs include trade promotion agreements (TPAs) such as the US–Peru TPA and the US–Panama TPA.
22. RIA levels of integration are discussed in Section 8.1.1.
23. The substantial transformation criterion is discussed in Chapter 2, Section 2.2.3.3.
24. This agreement is discussed in Chapter 2, Section 2.2.3.2.
25. The value-added method for determining substantial transformation is discussed in Chapter 2, Section 2.2.3.3.
26. ASEAN, *Operational Certification Procedures*, Article 3, Origin Criteria, (ii) and (iii).
27. In NAFTA, rules of origin are also called *marking rules*.
28. HS codes are discussed in Chapter 2, Section 2.2.2.
29. The HTSUSA is also called the "NAFTA preference rules."
30. The change-in-tariff-classification method is discussed in Chapter 2, Section 2.2.3.3.
31. US Customs and Border Protection, *About NAFTA and Textiles*, 12.
32. Organizational and functional mechanisms are discussed in Chapter 6, Section 6.4.
33. The integration continuum is discussed in Section 8.1.1.
34. NAFTA secretariat.
35. ASEAN FTA secretariat.
36. GCC, Implementation Procedures.
37. The CETA is discussed in Chapter 2, Section 2.3.2.2.
38. Bilateral FTAs are discussed in Section 8.6.
39. For example, two GCC CU member states (Bahrain and Oman) have entered into separate bilateral trade agreements (with the United States).
40. Some elements of the EU's organizational mechanism are discussed in Section 8.1.1.
41. This provision of the MA is discussed in Chapter 7, Section 7.4.2.1.
42. Because FTAs do not satisfy the definition contained in Article XX of the MA, they are not separate customs territories and cannot be members of the WTO.
43. The Treaty of Amity and Commerce and the Treaty of Alliance were signed in Paris on February 6, 1778.
44. Functional mechanisms are discussed in Chapter 6, Section 6.4.2.
45. This exception to Article I of the GATT is discussed in Section 8.2.2.
46. TPAs are discussed in Endnote 21.

9 The harmonization of laws and the settlement of disputes

Contents

9.1 The harmonization of laws

When a company is engaged in the conduct of IB, it is operating in more than one nation-state and more than one legal jurisdiction, and is subject to more than one set of legal principles and laws.

9.1.1 Legal jurisdiction

The conduct of IB includes the use of contracts that are entered into in different jurisdictions, that are between parties from different jurisdictions, and that govern the operations of companies in different jurisdictions.

The issue of legal jurisdiction can be problematic for companies engaged in the conduct of IB because companies engaged in international trade must comply simultaneously with the laws of exporting and importing countries, and companies engaged in FDI must comply simultaneously with the laws of their home country and the laws of their host country or countries. These conditions can be compounded and made more complex when a company has entered into multiple international contracts covered by multiple jurisdictions, operates in multiple nation-states and multiple legal systems, and is subject to multiple sets of legal principles and multiple sets of laws.[1]

Each of these conditions can be more problematic if there are differences in the laws in different jurisdictions.

9.1.2 The conflict of laws

Differences in the laws of different jurisdictions that affect individuals and corporations are referred to as the *conflict of laws*.

9.1.2.1 In domestic law

In domestic law, the conflict of laws occurs within nation-states that use a federal system, because these nation-states (which include Australia, Canada, and the US) have multiple jurisdictions.

9.1.2.2 In international law

In international law, the term *conflict of laws* refers to the differences in the laws of different jurisdictions, to the procedural rules that govern the use of laws from different jurisdictions, to how courts determine which of these laws apply to a specific dispute, and to the efforts by nation-states and intergovernmental organizations to reduce the adverse effects of conflicting laws.

The term is also used when referring to the body of conventions, model laws, legal guidelines, and other agreements between nation-states that are designed to reduce or to bridge differences in the laws of individual nation-states—which affect the international activities of individuals and corporations.

The *conflict of laws* can also be seen as a process for harmonizing the laws of separate nation-states, and for developing a consensus among nation-states relating to laws that affect the international activities of individuals and the operations of corporations.

9.1.3 Synonyms and distinctions

1. *Private international law*: The body of international law that governs the relationships between nation-states is referred to as *public international law*. To differentiate between public international law and the differences in the laws that affect the international activities of individuals and the international operations of corporations, the conflict of laws is referred to as *private international law*.[2]
2. *Choice of laws*: Because conflict-of-laws procedures and agreements govern which law applies in a particular situation, the conflict of laws is also referred to as the *choice of laws*.

3. *Harmonization of laws*: And, finally, because the conflict of laws refers to the efforts by nation-states and intergovernmental organizations to reduce the adverse effects of conflicting laws, it is also referred to as the *harmonization of laws*.

The term *harmonization* is sometimes used in the area of public international law. For example, the word *harmonization* is used in the text of the Agreement on Rules of Origin, and in the title and text of the International Convention on the Simplification and Harmonization of Customs Procedures.[3] The term *harmonization of laws*, however, is a synonym for the *conflict of laws* and *private international law*.

9.1.4 Instruments and mechanisms for the harmonization of laws

The harmonization of laws is effected through the work of intergovernmental organizations and through intergovernmental instruments that have been signed and ratified by nation-states.

9.1.4.1 Private international law instruments

Instruments for the harmonization of laws include:

1. United Nations Convention on Contracts for the International Sale of Goods
2. Convention on the Recognition and Enforcement of Foreign Arbitral Awards
3. Convention on Stolen or Illegally Exported Cultural Objects
4. Convention on International Interests in Mobile Equipment
5. Convention on the Service Abroad of Judicial and Extrajudicial Documents in Civil or Commercial Matters
6. Convention on the Taking of Evidence Abroad in Civil or Commercial Matters

9.1.4.2 Private international law mechanisms

There are several intergovernmental organizations that focus solely on, or whose work includes, the harmonization of laws.

UNCITRAL

The United Nations Commission on International Trade Law was established by the General Assembly of the United Nations in 1966, for the purpose of "modernizing and harmonizing the rules on international business." UNCITRAL has developed more than 40 intergovernmental instruments in the field of international trade law and commercial law reform.

The first two instruments on the list in Section 9.1.4.1 were created under the auspice of UNCITRAL.[4]

UNIDROIT

The International Institute for the Unification of Private Law was created in 1926 as an organ of the League of Nations. UNIDROIT is now an autonomous intergovernmental organization for "modernizing, harmonizing and coordinating private and in particular commercial law."

Instruments 3 and 4 on the list in Section 9.1.4.1 were created under the auspices of UNIDROIT.[5]

HCCH

The first Hague Conference on Private International Law was held in 1893; in 1955 it became a permanent intergovernmental organization. HCCH develops and services multilateral legal instruments for the purpose of achieving the "progressive unification" of private international law relating to "personal, family and commercial situations."

Instruments 5 and 6 on the list in Section 9.1.4.1 were created under the auspice of the HCCH.

9.1.4.3 The US and the harmonization of laws

The US became a member of UNCITRAL in 1966, of UNIDROIT in 1964, and of HCCH in 1964. The US has ratified all of the instruments listed in Section 9.1.4.1.

9.2 International business disputes

International disputes can be classified by: (1) the subject of the dispute, (2) the identity of the parties to the dispute, and (3) the law or laws that are applicable to the dispute.

9.2.1 The subject of the dispute

In the conduct and study of IR, the subject of a dispute can be classified as political, security-related, or commercial.

Other subject classifications include territory, ideology, religion, and human rights. These subject classifications are in some cases seen as sub-categories of political or security-related disputes. Also, some international disputes defy single-category classification because they cover two or more subject categories.

International commercial disputes can be classified as either trade disputes or investment disputes. The term *investment disputes* refers to disputes related to FDI.

9.2.2 The parties to the dispute

The parties to international commercial disputes can be divided into two primary categories: *nation-states* and *nationals of nation-states*.[6] For example: Japan is a nation-state; Toyota is a national of a nation-state.

The term *nationals of nation-states* includes individuals, corporations, and non-governmental organizations. The division between nation-states and nationals of nation-states results in three types of international commercial disputes.

1. Disputes between nation-states
2. Disputes between nationals of different nation-states
3. Disputes between nation-states and nationals of other nation-states

9.2.2.1 Disputes between nation-states

The dispute between Brazil and the US over subsidies the US government pays to US cotton farmers is a dispute between nation-states.[7]

9.2.2.2 Disputes between nationals of different nation-states

**DVD manufacturers in China and
non-Chinese owners of DVD technology**

From 2000 to 2006, Chinese companies that manufacture DVD players were engaged in a dispute with Japanese, European, and US companies that own DVD technology (including Hitachi, Panasonic, Mitsubishi, Toshiba, JVC, Philips, Sony, and Pioneer) over the payment of royalties. This was a dispute between nationals of different nation-states.

9.2.2.3 Disputes between nation-states and nationals of other nation-states

The EU and DVD manufacturers in China

The dispute over royalty payments for the use of DVD technology led the European Union to block the importation of Chinese-made DVD players. This resulted in a dispute between the EU and the Chinese companies that manufacture DVD players.

Because the EU is a separate customs territory, this dispute is seen as being between a nation-state (the EU) and nationals of another nation-state (the Chinese manufacturers of DVD players).

9.2.3 Applicable law

Article 1, Paragraph 1, of the UN Charter says the settlement of international disputes should be "in conformity with the principles of justice and international law."

The type of applicable law can be determined by the identity of the parties to the dispute, by the subject of the dispute, and/or by the location of the dispute.

9.2.3.1 Nation-states

If the parties to a dispute are nation-states, the applicable law may be customary international law or treaty law.

1. *Customary international law*: The sources of customary international law used by the International Court of Justice include "international custom, as evidence of a general practice accepted as law,… general principles of law recognized by civilized nations,… judicial decisions," and the teachings of eminent legal scholars.[8] Customary international law can also include treaty law that over time has become "international custom, as evidence of a general practice accepted as law."

2. *Treaty law*: The term *treaty law* refers to law that comes from one or more international instruments. Because the source of treaty law is instruments, which are written agreements, it is sometimes referred to as *black letter law*.[9]

Japan and Ukraine: Safeguards

In 2013, Japan brought a complaint to the WTO Dispute Settlement Body against Ukraine "regarding the definitive safeguard measures[10] imposed by Ukraine on imports of certain passenger cars and the investigation that led to the imposition of those measures."[11]

In this action, Japan claimed the measures taken by Ukraine were "inconsistent with Articles 2.1, 3.1, 4.1(a), 4.1(b), 4.2(a), 4.2(b), 4.2(c), 5.1, 7.1, 7.4, 8.1, 11.1(a), 12.1, 12.2 and 12.3 of the Agreement on Safeguards; and with Articles II:1(b) and XIX:1(a) of the GATT 1994."

Japan's action was based on specific provisions of agreements to which Japan and Ukraine are parties, and was, therefore, a use of treaty law—or black letter law.

9.2.3.2 Nationals of different nation-states

If the parties to a dispute are companies that are nationals of different nation-states, the applicable law is the laws of the nation-state in which the disputed action has occurred—unless there is a prior written agreement between the parties to use an extra-national alternative.[12]

These extra-national alternatives are discussed in Section 9.3.2. As discussed in Section 9.3.2.3, the use of extra-national alternatives can be subject to restrictions.

9.2.3.3 Nation-states and nationals of other nation-states

If the parties to a dispute are the government of a nation-state and a company that is a national of another state, the dispute is governed by the laws of the nation-state in which the disputed action has occurred—unless there is a prior written agreement between the parties that provides for the use of an extra-national alternative.

These extra-national alternatives are discussed in Section 9.3.3.

9.2.3.4 The conflict of laws

In some IB disputes, the applicable law can include laws of the company's host-country and home-country.[13] If there are differences in applicable home-country and host-country laws, this can result in the conflict of laws.[14]

9.2.4 The need for international DSMs

The processes and mechanisms used in the settlement of domestic commercial disputes are, in most cases, unsuitable for the settlement of international commercial disputes.[15]

9.2.4.1 For national governments

Commercial disputes between nation-states cannot be settled using the courts and laws of either nation-state that is a party to a dispute, because the legal playing field would not be level.

Brazil and the US: Subsidies

The dispute between Brazil and the US, over subsidies the US government pays to US cotton farmers cannot be settled using the courts of Brazil or the United States.

9.2.4.2 For companies

The legal dictum *locus regit actum* says disputes should be decided using the courts and laws of the location where the disputed action has occurred. But for companies engaged in the conduct of IB, the use of a host-country's courts and laws can be problematic—because the legal playing field may not be level.

1. *Nationals of different nation-states*: In disputes between nationals of different nation-states, there can be a problem using the courts of the country where the dispute has occurred—if one party to the dispute is a foreign national[16] and the other party is a national of the host-country. In these cases, the legal playing field may not be level because the host-country national may receive preferential treatment by the host country's courts.
2. *Nation-states and nationals of other nation-states*: In disputes between nation-states and nationals of other nation-states, the legal playing field may not be level because the host-country government may receive preferential treatment by the host country's courts.

9.3 Dispute settlement mechanisms

The term *dispute settlement mechanism* (DSM) refers to a mechanism that can be used to facilitate the resolution of a dispute.

DSMs are characterized by several criteria, which include: (1) the parties that are permitted to use the DSM, (2) the organization within which the DSM is located, (3) the subject areas covered by the DSM, (4) the types of law applied by the DSM, (5) the DSM's geographical scope, and (6) the dispute settlement procedures offered by the DSM.[17]

DSMs that are used to facilitate the resolution of international trade and foreign investment disputes can, like types of disputes, be grouped into three categories:

1. DSMs for the settlement of disputes between nation-states
2. DSMs for the settlement of disputes between nationals of different nation-states
3. DSMs for the settlement of disputes between nation-states and nationals of other nation-states

Most DSMs for the settlement of international commercial disputes are sub-units of global or regional intergovernmental organizations.

9.3.1 DSMs for disputes between nation-states

DSMs that are used to settle international commercial disputes between nation-states can be classified as trade related or not-trade related, and as global or regional.

9.3.1.1 The WTO Dispute Settlement Body

The principal global DSM for the settlement of trade-related disputes between nation-states is the WTO Dispute Settlement Body (DSB).

The WTO Dispute Settlement Body is discussed in Section 9.5.

9.3.1.2 Other global DSMs for disputes between nation-states

Economic and commercial disputes that are not related to trade can be decided by the International Court of Justice or by a subject-specific DSM.

Off-shore oil and gas reserves

Some nation-states have used the ICJ to settle disputes over off-shore oil and gas reserves. Other nation-states have taken these disputes to the International Tribunal for the Law of the Sea, which was created by the United Nations Convention on the Law of the Sea (UNCLOS).

9.3.1.3 Regional DSMs for disputes between nation-states

Some of the regional trade blocs that are discussed in Chapter 8, Section 8.2, have established mechanisms for settling disputes between their member states.

- The ASEAN Free Trade Area's DSM was established by the ASEAN Protocol on Enhanced Dispute Settlement Mechanism of 1996 and 2004.
- The Economic Community of West African States (ECOWAS)[18] has established a Court of Justice for handling economic disputes between ECOWAS member states.
- The MERCOSUR Common Market Group[19] and the North American Free Trade Agreement have DSMs for settling commercial disputes.

The development and use of regional DSMs is supported by the UN Charter. The list of procedures contained in Article 33 of the charter includes the use of "regional agencies or arrangements."[20]

9.3.2 DSMs for disputes between nationals of different nation-states

Disputes between companies that are nationals of different nation-states must be settled using the courts and laws of the nation-state in which the dispute occurs—unless the contractual agreement between the parties to the dispute provides for the use of an extra-national dispute settlement mechanism.

There are two types of extra-national alternatives: third-country and institutional options.

9.3.2.1 Third-country options

Some companies state in their contractual agreements that, in the case of a dispute, they will use the courts and laws of a third country.

China, the US, and Sweden: Pepsi

The agreement between PepsiCo (a US company) and its Chinese equity joint venture partner in Chengdu, Sichuan Province, designated the Court of Commercial Arbitration in Stockholm as the forum for the settlement of disputes.[21]

In some cases, the third-country option employs the courts of one third country and the laws of another third country.

9.3.2.2 Institutional options

The contractual agreements between some companies state that, in the case of a dispute, they will use a specific international DSM that has been established for the purpose of settling disputes between nationals of different nation-states.

These DSMs include:

- International Court of Arbitration,[22] which is the dispute-settlement body of the International Chamber of Commerce (ICC)
- Arbitration and Mediation Center of the World Intellectual Property Organization[23]

9.3.2.3 The exhaustion of local remedies

Some nation-states require that companies that are parties to a dispute must use the full range of procedures offered by their country's courts before taking a dispute to an extra-national dispute settlement mechanism. This requirement is called *the exhaustion of local remedies.*

Even where a nation-state does not require the exhaustion of local remedies, the parties to a dispute may be required to have local courts approve that the dispute be decided by an extra-national DSM.

China, the US, and Sweden: Pepsi

In 2003, PepsiCo brought a legal action against its Chinese equity joint venture partner in Chengdu, Sichuan Province, over mismanagement, financial irregularities, and control.

This dispute was first submitted to Chengdu courts, which (1) approved the dispute-settlement clause contained in the EJV agreement and (2) approved that the dispute be decided by the Court of Commercial Arbitration in Stockholm.

9.3.3 DSMs for disputes between nation-states and nationals of other nation-states

Disputes between nation-states and nationals of other nation-states must be settled using the courts and laws of the nation-state in which the dispute occurs—unless the FDI agreement between the company and the host-country government includes a *compromissory clause* that provides for the use of an extra-national dispute settlement mechanism, or unless this provision is included in a governing bilateral or multilateral agreement.

9.3.3.1 ISDS

Since the 1960s, an increasing number of bilateral and multilateral trade and investment agreements have included extra-national procedures for the settlement of disputes between nation-states and nationals of other nation-states. The dispute-settlement articles of these agreements are referred to generically as Investor-State Dispute Settlement (ISDS) clauses.

The Office of the US Trade Representative says that "various forms of ISDS are now a part of over 3,000 agreements worldwide, of which the United States is party to 50."[24]

NAFTA

Chapter 11 of NAFTA provides for the use of extra-national arbitration using the ICSID Convention, the Additional Facility Rules of ICSID, or the UNCITRAL Arbitration Rules, and waives the exhaustion-of-local-remedies requirement if the host country "has deprived a disputing investor of control of an enterprise."[25]

9.3.3.2 ICSID

The most widely used mechanism for the settlement of disputes between nation-states and nationals of other nation-states is the International Center for the Settlement of Investment Disputes.[26]

ICSID was created by the World Bank in 1966.[27] As of 2014, the Convention on the Settlement of Investment Disputes between States and Nationals of Other States had been signed by 158 states and ratified by 150 states.[28] Three former contracting states, Bolivia, Ecuador, and Venezuela, have withdrawn from the convention.

As of 2014, ICSID had accepted more than 390 cases, of which about 250 have been concluded.

9.3.3.3 Third-country options

Foreign-funded companies and the governments of host-countries have also chosen to use the third-country option.[29]

Peru and Japan: Swedish courts

The compromissory clause in an agreement between a Japanese oil pipeline construction company and the government of Peru provided that, in the case of a dispute, the parties would use Swedish courts and UK law.

9.4 Dispute settlement procedures

The term *dispute settlement procedures* refers to the methods used to settle disputes.

International dispute settlement procedures are characterized by (1) the availability of a large number of different procedures and (2) the diversity of these procedures.

9.4.1 The underlying principle

Article 33 of the UN Charter[30] says:

> The parties to any dispute, the continuance of which is likely to endanger the maintenance of international peace and security, shall, first of all, seek a solution by negotiation, enquiry, mediation, conciliation, arbitration, judicial settlement, resort to regional agencies or arrangements, or other peaceful means of their own choice.

The procedures listed in this text are arranged, more or less, in hierarchical order:[31] from procedures that are less adversarial to procedures that are more adversarial.

Article 33 of the charter, and especially the phrase "shall, first of all, seek a solution," is seen as containing the principle that parties to a dispute should seek a solution at the lowest adversarial level.

Although the text of Article 33 refers to disputes related to "international peace and security," the practice of using the least adversarial procedure has come to influence all areas of international dispute settlement, including the settlement of commercial disputes.

Also, although Article 33 addresses the settlement of disputes between nation-states, the principle contained in this article is applied by DSMs that are used by nationals of nation-states.

9.4.2 The six-procedure hierarchy

The procedures used to settle international disputes, including international commercial disputes, can be arranged in a six-element hierarchy.

1. Negotiation/consultation
2. Good offices
3. Conciliation
4. Mediation
5. Arbitration
6. Adjudication/litigation

This hierarchy begins with the procedure that is least adversarial—followed by procedures that are increasingly more adversarial.

9.4.2.1 Negotiation/consultation

The primary characteristics of negotiation or consultation are that the procedure (1) is non-binding and (2) does not involve the participation of a third party. This procedure does not result in a legal conclusion, but assists the parties to reach a mutually acceptable solution.

The terms *negotiation* and *consultation* are often used interchangeably. There has, however, been an increase in the use of the term *consultation*, because consultation is the first step in the WTO dispute settlement system.[32]

9.4.2.2 Good offices

The good offices procedure is similar to negotiation and consultation, but includes the participation of a third party. An important characteristic of good offices, however, is that the third party facilitates the meeting of the parties to the dispute—but does not participate in the negotiations or consultations.

9.4.2.3 Conciliation

The conciliation procedure is similar to good offices, but the *conciliator* participates in the negotiation and consultation process. The role of the conciliator, however, is limited—and the conciliator is not positioned between the parties to the dispute. In the conciliation procedure, the two parties are still discussing the situation directly, and the role of the conciliator is to facilitate the process.

9.4.2.4 Mediation

Mediation is similar to conciliation, but the *mediator* is positioned between the parties to the dispute. Also, in mediation, the mediator may propose a solution to the parties.

9.4.2.5 Arbitration

Arbitration also uses the participation of a third party, called the *arbitrator*. In arbitration: (1) the parties to the dispute do not engage in negotiation or consultation, but present their arguments to the arbitrator; (2) the procedure results in a legal conclusion; and (3) the legal conclusion is binding.

Arbitration is not, however, a judicial procedure: It does not take place in a court of law and is not subject to strict legal structures and requirements. Because of this, an arbitrator has more flexibility than a judge when deciding how a procedure is handled, how a decision is reached, and the terms and scope of the decision.

9.4.2.6 Adjudication/litigation

Adjudication, which is also called *litigation*, shares some similarities with arbitration: It results in a legal conclusion, and the decision of the judge (or judges) is binding upon the parties to the dispute.

The difference, however, is that adjudication/litigation is a judicial procedure. It takes place in a court of law and is subject to strict legal structures and requirements.

9.4.3 Dispute settlement procedures offered by DSMs

Most of the dispute settlement mechanisms discussed in Sections 9.3 and 9.5 support the principle of seeking a solution at the lowest adversarial level by offering at least two procedures and/or by requiring that the parties first attempt to resolve the dispute through negotiation or consultation.

- The Arbitration and Mediation Center of the WIPO offers mediation and arbitration procedures.
- ICSID offers conciliation and arbitration.
- Article 23 of the ASEAN Charter says that "parties to the dispute may request the Chairman of ASEAN or the Secretary-General of ASEAN, acting in an ex-officio capacity, to provide good offices, conciliation or mediation."
- The WTO Dispute Settlement Body offers five dispute settlement procedures, which are discussed in Section 9.5.3, and requires that consultation be the first step in resolving a dispute when using the DSB.
- Chapter 11 of NAFTA says that "The disputing parties should first attempt to settle a claim through consultation or negotiation."[33]

9.5 The WTO Dispute Settlement Body

The DSB was created by the 1994 Uruguay Round Understanding on Rules and Procedures Governing the Settlement of Disputes, which is commonly referred to as the Dispute Settlement Understanding, as the 1994 Understanding,[34] or simply as the Understanding.

Article 1, Paragraph 1, says the rules and procedures of the Understanding shall apply to consultations and the settlement of disputes between WTO Members.

The DSB can, however, also be used by nation-states and by separate customs territories that are not WTO members—if both parties to the dispute agree to use the mechanism.

9.5.1 Applicable law

Article 1, Paragraph 1, says the Understanding applies to "disputes brought pursuant to the consultation and dispute settlement provisions of the agreements listed in Appendix 1." Because the disputes handled by the DSB are based on provisions contained in instruments, the DSB uses treaty law.[35]

Articles 3 and 27 of the Understanding refer to "provisions of…agreements in accordance with customary rules of interpretation of public international law"[36] and "historical…aspects of the matters dealt with"—which indicate the DSB's decisions may also be influenced by customary international law.[37]

9.5.2 Functional mechanisms

The WTO DSB is characterized by a unique dispute settlement system, which has three functional mechanisms: (1) panels, (2) the Appellate Body, and (3) the DSB.

This system was developed by the GATT organization and the GATT Secretariat between 1948 and 1994. The system was codified and modified during the Tokyo Round (1973–1979) and Uruguay Round (1986–1994) of multilateral trade negotiations.[38]

9.5.2.1 Panels

In 1952, the GATT began to use panels to investigate complaints by contracting parties. The term *panel* was used to emphasize the technical objectivity of the persons engaged in these investigations. The panels, their composition, and their terms of operation have been subject to many changes[39]—and they have evolved into the panel procedure that is detailed in Articles 6 to 16 of the 1994 Understanding.

Article 6 of the Understanding says that, at the request of a "complaining party,"[40] the Secretariat of the DSB will establish an ad hoc panel (composed of three persons) to make an objective assessment of the dispute and to report findings and conclusions to the DSB.

9.5.2.2 The Appellate Body

Article 17 provides for the establishment of a standing Appellate Body, and that "parties to the dispute…may appeal a panel report."

The Appellate Body is composed of seven persons, each of whom is appointed to a four-year term, and "three of whom shall serve on any one case." Appeals are "limited to issues of law covered in the panel report and legal interpretations developed by the panel."[41] "The Appellate Body may uphold, modify or reverse the legal findings and conclusions of the panel."[42]

9.5.2.3 *The DSB*

As discussed in Chapter 7, Section 7.4.1.2, all members of the WTO are members of the Dispute Settlement Body. Any reference to the DSB means, therefore, all members of the WTO.

Article 15 of the Understanding, Interim Review Stage, allows for the parties to a dispute to make comments on a panel report, following which "the final panel report" will be circulated to Members.

Article 16, Adoption of Panel reports, says that following the circulation of a report, and absent an appeal by a party to the dispute, the panel report will be adopted by the DSB. Article 17, Paragraph 14, says reports by the Appellate Body "shall be adopted by the DSB and unconditionally accepted by the parties to the dispute."

Article 21 includes measures for the prompt and effective implementation of and compliance with the DSB's recommendations and/or rulings.

9.5.3 *WTO DSB procedures*

The dispute settlement procedures offered by the WTO DSB are consultation, good offices, conciliation, mediation, arbitration, and the panels and Appellate Review system.

9.5.3.1 *Consultation*

Article 3, General Provisions, of the Understanding says that WTO Members "affirm their adherence" to the principles, rules, and procedures for the management of disputes contained in Articles XXII and XXIII of GATT 1947.

Article XXII, Consultation, of GATT 1947 provides for consultation between the contracting parties "with respect to any matter affecting the operation of this Agreement."

Article 4, Consultations, of the 1994 Understanding repeats the "consultation" language from the GATT, and provides extensive details concerning the use of the consultation procedure. These details cover notifying the DSB, the confidentiality of consultations, and the times allowed for responding to a request for consultation.

9.5.3.2 *Good offices, conciliation, and mediation*

Article 5 of the Understanding says that "good offices, conciliation or mediation may be requested at any time by any party to a dispute" and that "if the parties to a dispute agree, procedures for good offices, conciliation or mediation may continue while the panel process proceeds."

9.5.3.3 *Arbitration*

Article 25 of the Understanding offers "expeditious arbitration within the WTO as an alternative means of dispute settlement" if both parties to a dispute agree to use this procedure and if the parties "agree to abide by the arbitration award."

9.5.3.4 Procedures used by panels and the Appellate Body

For disputes that are not resolved through consultation, the DSB's principal elements are the procedures offered by its panels and Appellate Review system.[43]

The 1994 Understanding does not address directly which of the six procedures discussed in Section 9.4.2 are used by the panels and the Appellate Body. But Article 12, Paragraphs 6 and 7, says the parties must submit their arguments to the panel, which then reports its findings and recommendations to the DSB; and Articles 16 and 17 discuss the adoption of panel and Appellate Body reports.

These articles of the Understanding indicate that the procedures used by the DSB panels and Appellate Review system are a form of arbitration,[44] except that, in each case, the role of arbitrator is divided between the panel and the DSB and, if there is an appeal, the Appellate Body.

9.5.4 Characteristics of the DSB system

There are three characteristics that distinguish the DSB system. The first is its range of dispute settlement alternatives. The second is its panels and Appellate Review system. The third is the emphasis on consultation.

The GATT and the 1994 Understanding designate consultation as the first step to be taken by a WTO member that has a complaint against another member.

Japan and Ukraine: Safeguards

In October 2013, when Japan initiated its complaint against Ukraine relating to the use of safeguard measures,[45] it requested consultations with Ukraine. In November 2013, the EU and Russia requested that they be allowed to join these consultations, and Ukraine informed the DSB it had accepted the requests by the EU and Russia.

Russia and the EU: Anti-dumping

In 2014, Russia issued "a request for consultations with the European Union regarding anti-dumping measures imposed by the European Union on several products imported from Russia, including ammonium nitrate and steel products,"[46] and notified the WTO Secretariat of this request.[47]

Because consultation has the lowest adversarial level of any of the procedures discussed in Section 9.4.2, this provision of GATT 1947 and the DSB is consistent with the principle contained in Article 33 of the UN Charter, of seeking a solution at the lowest adversarial level.

Due to this emphasis on the use of consultation, more than half of the disputes brought to the DSB have been resolved without reaching the panel level.

9.5.5 Purpose

The purpose of the procedures offered by the DSB is not to penalize a member for not complying with the WTO's rules or requirements—or to compensate the complainant. Rather, the purpose is to resolve the dispute and, if possible, to find a mutually acceptable solution—or at least to remove the cause of the dispute. The Understanding says:

> The aim of the dispute settlement mechanism is to secure a positive solution to a dispute. A solution mutually acceptable to the parties to a dispute and consistent with the covered agreements is clearly to be preferred.
>
> In the absence of a mutually agreed solution, the first objective of the dispute settlement mechanism is usually to secure the withdrawal of the measures concerned if these are found to be inconsistent with the provisions of any of the covered agreements.[48]
>
> Where a panel or the Appellate Body concludes that a measure is inconsistent with a covered agreement, it shall recommend that the Member concerned bring the measure into conformity with that agreement.[49]

Endnotes

1. The effects of these conditions on the operations and management of companies engaged in the conduct of IB are discussed in Chapter 10, Section 10.1.2.
2. The usage of these two terms varies by country: *conflict of laws* is used more in Australia, Canada, the UK, and the US; *private international law* is used more in continental European countries and in countries in Africa and Latin America.
3. These instruments are discussed in Chapter 2, Section 2.2.3.2.
4. UNCITRAL is located in Vienna.
5. UNIDROIT is located in Rome.
6. As discussed in Chapter 6, Section 6.1.1.3, references to nation-states and nationals of nation-states include separate customs territories and nationals or residents of separate customs territories.
7. This dispute is discussed in Chapter 3, Section 3.2.4.3.
8. ICJ Statute, Article 38(1). Because the sources of "customary international law" include the body of precedent established in judicial decisions, it is similar to domestic common law.
9. International *treaty law* is similar to domestic *statute law*, because the source of treaty law is specific citable instruments.
10. Safeguards are discussed in Chapter 2, Section 2.3.2.3.
11. Press release, Dispute Settlement Japan–Ukraine.
12. The prefix *extra* in the term *extra-national* means "outside of."
13. The terms *home country* and *host country* are discussed in Chapter 6, Section 6.1.1.2.
14. The conflict of laws is discussed in Section 9.1.2.
15. The exception to this generalization is the use of third-country courts, which is discussed in Sections 9.3.2.1 and 9.3.3.2.
16. The term *foreign national* is discussed in Chapter 5, Endnote 13; and in Chapter 6, Section 6.1.1.2.

17. Dispute settlement procedures are discussed in Section 9.4. The dispute settlement procedures offered by DSMs are discussed in Section 9.4.3.
18. ECOWAS has 16 member states.
19. MERCOSUR member states are Argentina, Brazil, Paraguay, and Uruguay.
20. The procedures listed in Article 33 of the UN Charter are discussed in Section 9.4.1.
21. In this example, Sweden is a third country because it is neither China nor the US.
22. The International Court of Arbitration is located in Paris.
23. The WIPO and its DSM are located Geneva.
24. USTR, *ISDS*.
25. NAFTA, Article 1121, 4.
26. ICSID is located in Washington, DC.
27. The World Bank is discussed in Chapter 7, Endnote 12.
28. The United States signed the ICSID Convention in 1965 and deposited its instrument of ratification in 1966.
29. Third-country options are discussed in Sections 9.3.2.1 and 9.3.3.2.
30. Article 33 is contained in Chapter VI: Pacific Settlement of Disputes.
31. An exact hierarchical ordering would be: enquiry, negotiation, conciliation, mediation, arbitration, and judicial settlement.
32. Consultation in the WTO DSB system is discussed in Sections 9.5.3.1 and 9.5.4.
33. NAFTA, Article 1118.
34. The term *1994 Understanding* is used to differentiate this instrument from the 1979 Understanding Regarding Notification, Consultation, Dispute Settlement and Surveillance.
35. Treaty law is discussed in Section 9.2.3.1.
36. The term *public international law* is discussed in Section 9.1.3.
37. Customary international law is discussed in Section 9.2.3.1.
38. The Tokyo Round and Uruguay Round of multilateral trade negotiations are discussed in Chapter 7, Sections 7.3.2.1 and 7.3.2.2.
39. Hudec, "WTO Dispute Settlement Procedure."
40. The term *complaining party* refers to a WTO Member that is bringing a complaint against another WTO Member.
41. 1994. Understanding, Article 17, Paragraph 6.
42. 1994. Understanding, Article 17, Paragraph 13.
43. Panels and the Appellate Body are discussed in Sections 9.5.2.1 and 9.5.2.2.
44. Arbitration is discussed in Section 9.4.2.5.
45. This complaint is discussed in Section 9.2.3.1.
46. Press release, Dispute Settlement Russia–EU.
47. This was the first dispute originated by Russia with the WTO DSB.
48. 1994 Understanding, Article 3, General Provisions, Paragraph 7.
49. 1994 Understanding, Article 19, Panel and Appellate Body Recommendations.

Section IV

Complicating elements

10 Systemic and cultural differences

Contents

10.1 Systemic differences

The term *systemic differences*, when applied to the IB environment, refers to differences in legal, financial, political, economic, and social systems in different countries—and to differences in the components of these systems, which include differences in currencies, laws, languages, and cultures.

As discussed in Chapter 1, Section 1.2.3, systemic differences neither regulate nor facilitate the conduct of international business. These elements can, however, make the conduct of IB more complex and difficult than the conduct of domestic business.

The elements in this section are discussed in approximate order of their operational significance.[1]

10.1.1 Differences in currencies

The world's nation-states use about 182 different currencies.[2] Differences in currencies can make IB financial functions more complex and difficult than similar functions in domestic business. The most affected financial functions include costing and pricing, contract negotiation and implementation, and the processing of international payments. Also, currency conversion fees add to the cost of the conduct of IB.

10.1.1.1 Exchange rates

The complexity, difficulty, and costs associated with currency differences are exacerbated because the exchange rates of currencies are continually changing.

When there is an extended period of time between the signing and completion of an IB agreement (due to the time taken to manufacture, process, and/or ship products— or due to the length of supply or services agreements), changes in exchange rates can change significantly the amount received by the supplying company or paid by the purchasing company.

Because it is impossible to predict accurately future exchange rates, currency differences can also be a cause of uncertainty in the conduct of IB. Hedging and other mechanisms can be used to limit exposure to exchange-rate risk and to offset the adverse effects of exchange-rate changes, but these mechanisms further increase the complexity, difficulty, and cost of IB operations.

10.1.1.2 Currency unions

Currency unions (which are also called *monetary unions*) are created by groups of nation-states to avoid the complexity, difficulty, costs, and uncertainty associated with currency differences, and to facilitate the conduct of trade and FDI between member states.

There are now about 16 formal and informal currency unions, which vary in size from 2 to 21 members. The Armenian dram, Israeli shekel, Singapore and Brunei dollar, and the Swiss franc currency unions each have 2 member states; the Indian rupee and the Pacific Financial Community (CFP) franc each have 3; the Australian dollar has 4; the New Zealand dollar has 5; the US dollar has 11; the Central African franc (CFA) has 14; and the European Monetary Union (EMU) euro has 19.[3]

10.1.1.3 Reserve currencies

A reserve currency is a currency that is held in significant quantities by national governments and financial institutions as part of their foreign exchange reserves. As of 2014, the composition of the total allocated foreign exchange reserves of national governments was: the US dollar, 62%; the euro, 24%; the UK's pound sterling, 4%; the Japanese yen, 4%; the Australian dollar, 1.6%; the Canadian dollar, 1.6%; and the Swiss franc, 0.3%.

If neither of the companies engaged in an IB transaction is located in a reserve currency country,[4] the complexity, difficulty, costs, and uncertainty associated with currency differences is further exacerbated because, in these cases, currency conversion is usually a two-step process that involves three currencies.[5]

From Kenyan shillings to Russian rubles

When a company in Kenya is paying for products or services from Russia, the Kenyan shillings must first be converted into US dollars, euros, or some other reserve currency, and then converted from the reserve currency into Russian rubles.

Companies located in a reserve currency country can avoid the complexity, difficulty, costs, and uncertainty associated with the two-step exchange process.

Some non-reserve currency countries (such as Brazil, China, and Russia) have entered into trade and investment agreements with a limited number of other countries that allow for the direct exchange of currencies. Because of these agreements, some companies that are engaged in the conduct of IB between non-reserve currency countries can avoid the two-step exchange process.

10.1.1.4 International transfer pricing

The term *transfer pricing* refers to the price at which materials, components, products, and services are transferred between (1) business units of the same company and (2) business units and their parent company. Transfer pricing is generally not problematic in the conduct of domestic business, because a parent company and its business units are all using the same currency and are operating within the same national tax jurisdiction.

International transfer pricing can, however, be problematic. Many multinational corporations use transfer pricing to make profits and losses from their international operations occur in the parent company's tax jurisdiction, so that losses in one or more host countries can be used to offset profits in other host countries. This use of international transfer pricing results in operating subsidiaries in host countries showing low or no profits and paying low or no taxes. This has caused transfer pricing to be a highly contentious issue between foreign direct investors and the governments of developing countries.

To reduce the financial complexity of international transfer pricing, companies frequently conduct their intra-company pricing, agreements, and payments in the parent company's home-country currency. But this method complicates the conduct of business for a company's foreign business units because the method requires that these business units use two currencies in their internal accounting operations.

10.1.2 Differences in laws

The differences in the business-related laws of different nation-states can make the conduct of IB more complex and difficult than the conduct of domestic business.

10.1.2.1 Legal complications and difficulties

In the conduct of domestic business, companies must comply with different laws when they are operating in different cities, provinces, or states. Within a single nation-state, however, the laws of each jurisdiction in most cases apply only to a company's operations in that jurisdiction—and there is a national-level authority and process for resolving the conflict of laws.[6]

In the conduct of IB, legal compliance can be more complex and difficult because: (1) companies engaged in international trade must comply simultaneously with the laws of exporting and importing countries, (2) companies engaged in FDI must comply simultaneously with the laws of their home and host countries,[7] (3) differences in the laws of different nation-states can result in the conflict of laws, and (4) there is no supra-national authority or process for resolving the conflict of laws.

As discussed in Chapter 9, Section 9.1.1, the requirements relating to the simultaneous compliance with the laws of two nation-states, and the difficulties relating to the conflict of laws of two nation-states, are further compounded when a company has entered into international contracts in multiple nation-states, with parties from multiple nation-states, and when the company operates in multiple nation-states.

There are many international instruments and several international mechanisms that are contributing to the harmonization of laws.[8] But companies engaged in the conduct of IB must still comply simultaneously with different, inconsistent, and sometimes contradictory laws that can complicate every area of IB from financial reporting to human resources management.

10.1.2.2 Managerial complications and difficulties

Differences in laws can make it difficult or impossible for companies to use global policies, strategies, organizational structures, or standards.[9]

In international management, the term *global* refers to (1) a policy, strategy, organizational structure, or standard that a company applies without modification in all parts of the world, (2) a company's use of the same manufacturing and marketing methods in all parts of the world, and (3) a product that a company markets, without modification, in all parts of the world.

Global policies, strategies, organizational structures, standards, and methods allow a company to use the same practices in all of its operations in all parts of the world; to facilitate the company-wide standardization of human resources management, including employee benefits, pay scales, and performance evaluation criteria and processes; to facilitate centralized control, planning, and decision making; and to facilitate the development of a unified corporate culture.

When used in R&D, product development, manufacturing, and marketing—global policies, strategies, organizational structures, standards, and methods can maximize the use of a company's resources; optimize productivity, technology transfer, and quality control; facilitate supply chain management, including component design, development, manufacturing, and distribution; facilitate product distribution and servicing; and provide economies of scale.

Differences in laws can force companies to use multi-domestic policies, strategies (including corporate, product, manufacturing, and marketing strategies), organizational structures, standards, and methods.

The term *multi-domestic* refers to a company's use of modified or different policies, strategies, organizational structures, and standards in different countries; to its use of modified or different manufacturing and marketing methods in different countries; and to the marketing of modified or different products in different countries.

10.1.3 Other systemic differences

Systemic differences also include differences in languages, legal systems, financial systems, political and economic systems, and social systems.

10.1.3.1 Differences in languages

There are literally thousands of different languages and dialects in the world, and language differences are frequently seen as a principal factor that distinguishes the conduct of IB from the conduct of domestic business.

It could be argued, however, that language differences (like the differences in laws) are not unique to the conduct of IB: A single nation-state can have more than one language, and many nation-states include hundreds of dialects.

The reason for including language differences as an element of the IB environment is that—for companies engaged in the conduct of IB, and especially for companies operating in a large number of different countries—language differences can add to the complexity and cost of internal and external communications, and can add to the difficulty and cost of managing a company's IB operations.

10.1.3.2 Differences in legal systems

Different countries use a wide range of different legal systems that are based on civil law, common law, or religious law—or on combinations of these fundamental classifications and their sub-classifications. National legal systems that are based on the same classification or combination can also have major differences, such as the differences between Roman law and Napoleonic law within civil law systems. And even national legal systems that are ostensibly the same, such as the classical sharia systems used by some Islamic countries, frequently include significant differences.

For companies engaged in the conduct of IB, differences in legal systems can exacerbate the complexities and difficulties associated with differences in laws, which are discussed in Section 10.1.2, and can increase the possibility of misunderstandings and disputes. Differences in legal systems can also exacerbate the conflict of laws,[10] which can protract and jeopardize the settlement of disputes.

10.1.3.3 Differences in financial systems

The most conspicuous financial-system differences that affect the conduct of IB are differences in currencies, which are discussed in Section 10.1.1.

Other financial-system differences that affect the conduct of IB include differences in the rules, procedures, and requirements that govern the convertibility of currencies; the international movement of funds; the preparation and filing of corporate tax returns; and international transfer pricing.[11]

10.1.3.4 Differences in political and economic systems

Every nation-state's political and economic systems are influenced by a unique mix of geographical, historical, religious, socio-cultural, economic, and ideological factors. These factors also influence a nation-state's relations with other nation-states and with intergovernmental organizations.

The differences in the political systems of nation-states can increase a foreign company's exposure to host-country and home-country political risk.[12]

Differences in economic systems can contribute to international disagreements related to the use of the surrogate third-country rule when determining normal value in anti-dumping cases[13] and to disputes related to the use of subsidies.[14]

10.1.3.5 Differences in social systems

A nation-state's political and economic systems—and the geographical, historical, religious, socio-cultural, economic, and ideological factors that influence these systems—also contribute to a nation-state's unique social system.

Differences in the social systems of nation-states make it necessary for companies engaged in the conduct of IB to modify their human resources policies and to modify their marketing strategies, content, and methods. Also, differences in religious holidays and observances, national holidays and festivals, and work weeks and weekends can complicate communications between companies and foreign governments—and can complicate inter-company and intra-company communications and operations.

Social-system differences include socio-cultural differences, which are discussed in Section 10.2.

10.1.4 The effects of systemic differences on the conduct of IB

Each of the systemic differences discussed in this section can make the conduct of IB more complex and difficult than the conduct of domestic business. In some cases, these systemic differences can also exacerbate the adverse effects of the post-entry barriers discussed in Chapter 5, which include currency, financial, and human resources restrictions and requirements; land-ownership restrictions; local content, export quota, and environmental impact requirements; and a company's exposure to political risk.

10.2 Cultural differences

The most frequently cited social-system differences that affect the conduct of IB are socio-cultural differences.

The term *socio-cultural differences* refers to differences in the values, beliefs, and preferences of persons from different societies, and to differences in the ways persons from different societies customarily think and behave.

Socio-cultural differences are a subcategory of social-system differences and are, therefore, systemic differences. In the conduct and study of IB, however, it is customary practice to treat socio-cultural differences as a separate category.

Socio-cultural differences are commonly referred to simply as *cultural differences*.

10.2.1 International cultural difference

There is a large body of scholarly and clinical research that indicates persons from different countries have different values, beliefs, priorities, and ways of thinking. These differences can cause managers and executives from different countries to behave differently when formulating and implementing policies and strategies, when they are engaged in negotiations and decision making, and when they are performing a wide range of other managerial and executive functions.

10.2.1.1 The flaw in the concept

The term *international cultural difference* is in fact a misnomer, because cultural differences are related to differences in the values, beliefs, preferences, and customary thinking and behaviors of persons from different societies—not from different nation-states.

A nation-state can include many societies, each of which can exhibit varying degrees of cultural difference. Also, societies in different nation-states can share the same or similar cultural characteristics. When referring to cultural differences we should, therefore, refer to societies and not to nation-states.

10.2.1.2 The legitimization of the concept

Although cultural differences are society-specific phenomena, there is a widely accepted practice of associating a group of cultural behaviors with the nationals of a particular nation-state—and of comparing the cultural behaviors of nationals from different nation-states. For example, in his seminal work, *Culture's Consequences, International Differences in Work-Related Values*, social psychologist Geert Hofstede uses *country* and *nationality* as the primary criteria when classifying cultural differences.[15]

The frequent and widespread use of country and nationality criteria by sociologists, social anthropologists, social psychologists, IB professors, managers, and executives when referring to cultural differences has led to the legitimization of the concept of international cultural difference.

10.2.1.3　The dichotomous pairs

International cultural differences are usually presented as dichotomous pairs,[16] with the elements of each pair defining the ends of a continuum.

Hofstede's Country Individualism

Hofstede used his research data to develop an individualist–collectivist dichotomy and a Country Individualism Index.[18] In this index, the US, Australia, and the UK are located close to the individualist end of the continuum; India, Japan, Brazil, and Turkey are located near the middle of the continuum; and Indonesia, Pakistan, and several Latin American countries (Colombia, Venezuela, Ecuador, and Guatemala) are located near the collectivist end of the continuum.[18]

Some cultural differences, such as "past, present, and future orientation," are referred to using a three-element classification. When this occurs, the first and third elements are a dichotomous pair and define the ends of a continuum; the second element refers to the middle area on the continuum.

10.2.2　Dichotomous pairs that influence the conduct of IB

10.2.2.1　Language–context

The elements of the language–context dichotomy, which were developed by Edward Hall,[19] are low-context language and high-context language.

Persons from low-context language societies, which include Germanic, Scandinavian, and Anglo countries (including the United States), include relatively large amounts of information in their communications, because they work in a social environment where there is no generally agreed-upon social text, and nothing can be assumed. Managers and executives from low-context language countries tend to try to cover every imaginable issue in their communications, and their negotiations can result in voluminous agreement documents.

Persons from high-context language societies, which include many Asian and Arab societies, omit information from their communications that is contained in their generally agreed-upon social text, because it is assumed that this information is already known by the recipient of the communication. Managers and executives from high-context language countries give more weight to the identity of the person who is speaking or writing; they focus more on the purpose and intent of communications; and they prefer brief agreement documents.

10.2.2.2 Power–distance

The elements of the power–distance dichotomy are high power distance and low power distance. The term *power distance* and its elements were developed by Hofstede.

Persons from high power-distance societies recognize and respect hierarchy. Managers and executives from high power–distance countries tend to be very conscious of their position in their company's organizational structure; defer to the values, beliefs, and opinions of their superiors; prefer to make recommendations to their superiors rather than to make decisions; and frequently seek input or permission from their superiors before taking actions.

Persons from low power–distance societies tend to be egalitarian in their philosophy, beliefs, and behavior. Managers and executives from low power–distance countries believe in flat organizational structures, and may not see the person to whom they report as a superior. These managers and executives believe they are responsible for evaluating situations, making decisions, and taking actions—with no or very limited input or permission from the person to whom they report.

10.2.2.3 Individualist–collectivist

As discussed in the example in Section 10.2.1.3, societies (and countries) can be classified using an individualist–collectivist continuum.

Persons from individualist societies believe strongly in the rights of the individual and prefer to act independently. Managers and executives from individualist countries frequently prefer to work alone. When faced with a decision, these managers and executives (and especially entrepreneurs and heads of small, medium-sized, and family-owned companies) may seek input from a group, but prefer to do their own assessments, evaluations, and decision making.

Persons from collectivist societies believe in the value of groups (and especially extended families), and prefer to do things as a member of a group. Managers and executives from collectivist societies enjoy and excel at working as part of a team or as a team leader; prefer that decisions be made by groups that include representatives from all affected constituencies and that decisions be made by consensus; and share responsibility for the implementation of decisions.

10.2.2.4 Uncertainty avoiding–uncertainty tolerant

Persons from uncertainty-avoiding societies tend to avoid situations where the outcome is unknown, or where there is a medium to high possibility of an unsatisfactory outcome, and tend to have a high fear of failure. Managers and executives from uncertainty-avoiding countries avoid career choices that are high risk, prefer positions in established companies in secure and non-cyclical industries, make conservative decisions, and prefer to avoid decisions that involve critical variables that defy projection.

Persons from uncertainty-tolerant societies are unconcerned by, and may even be stimulated and/or motivated by, situations where the outcome is unknown and where there is a high possibility of failure. Managers and executives from uncertainty-tolerant countries prefer high-risk high-reward career paths (such as working as an entrepreneur, for a start-up, or in a new industry), volunteer for assignments in foreign or troubled business units, and enjoy making difficult and bold decisions.

10.2.2.5 Competition–cooperation

In some societies, and especially Western societies, there is a high emphasis on competition, and competition is believed to be a universally beneficial phenomenon. In these societies, competition is seen as a central factor in the creation and operation of a free market economy, and in the creation and delivery of a wide range of products and services, better customer service, and lower prices. These societies use competition as the mechanism to rank success and to allocate recognition and rewards in every area from sports and education to politics and business.

In other societies, and especially in Asian countries and countries that use socialist governmental and political systems, there is an awareness of and aversion to the potentially negative effects of competition; a high emphasis on cooperation, collaboration, and harmony; and a belief that cooperation is mutually beneficial for society and for all members of society. Managers and executives from these countries favor the use of plus-sum[20] solutions when solving problems, prefer plus-sum policies and strategies, tend to work well in teams, and excel in strategic alliances.

10.2.2.6 Ambiguity tolerant–ambiguity averse

This dichotomous pair is in some ways similar to the uncertainty avoiding–uncertainty tolerant pair, because both of these pairs refer to being comfortable or uncomfortable with the unknown.

Societies are not, however, consistent in the preferences they exhibit in both of these pairs.

The US and China

As a society the United States tends to be uncertainty tolerant, but is fiercely averse to ambiguity.

As a society China is comfortable with and enjoys ambiguity, but fiercely avoids uncertainty.

10.2.2.7 Process oriented–results oriented

There is an essential causal relationship between *process* and *results*. These two elements can, however, form a cultural dichotomous pair—because managers, executives, and companies from different countries give varying degrees of emphasis to these two elements.

TQM and Six Sigma

In Japan, process orientation and the belief in continuous improvement (Kaizen) resulted in Toyota's development of the quality improvement processes called Total Quality Control (TQC) or Total Quality Management (TQM). In the US, results orientation and the need to reduce manufacturing errors resulted in Motorola's development of the defects measurement system called Six Sigma.[21]

10.2.2.8 Masculine–feminine

Decisions and actions by managers and executives from masculine societies are more influenced by professional and career factors.

Decisions and actions by managers and executives from feminine societies are more influenced by personal and family factors.[22]

10.2.2.9 Abstractive thinking–associative thinking; normative thinking–situational thinking

Persons from abstractive-thinking and normative-thinking societies are comfortable learning or discussing concepts, principles, or theories—without associating them with examples or cases.

Persons from associative-thinking and situational-thinking societies have great difficulty learning or discussing concepts, principles, or theories—unless they are associated with examples or cases.

10.2.2.10 Other dichotomous pairs that can affect the conduct of IB

The conduct of IB can also be affected by other cultural dichotomous pairs, which include: short term–long term, trust–distrust, nuclear families–extended families, indulgence–restraint, inductive thinking–deductive thinking; and by the three-element past, present, and future orientation.

10.2.3 The effects of cultural differences on the conduct of IB

Some cultural differences have a relatively low adverse effect on the conduct of IB, or their effects are relatively manageable.

When managers and executives from the same company or the same business unit are from countries that are at or near opposite ends of cultural continua, this can result in a wide range of differing opinions and expectations related to managerial methods, decision making, communication, and accountability. In most cases, however, the potential adverse effects of these differences can be offset by the company's operating policies and corporate culture.

10.2.3.1 Positive effects

In some situations, the operational significance of cultural elements can be positive, and a combination of cultural elements can be highly positive.

The positive effects on the operations of ISAs

Managers and executives from countries that are at or near the high-context language, collectivist, cooperation, long term, process oriented, and trust ends of cultural continua tend to work exceptionally well in international strategic alliances (ISAs).[23]

When the partner companies of an ISA are from countries that are at or near these ends of cultural continua, there is a reduced probability of intramural competition within the ISA and a reduced exposure to partner risk,[24] which improves the ISA's operational effectiveness and sustainability.

10.2.3.2 Negative effects

In some situations, the operational significance of cultural elements can be negative or highly negative.

The negative effects on the operations of ISAs

If the managers and executives in an ISA are from countries that are at or near the low-context language, individualist, competition, short term, results oriented, and distrust ends of cultural continua—or if the partner companies of an ISA are from countries that are at or near these ends of cultural continua— this can increase the probability of intramural competition within the ISA and can adversely affect its operational effectiveness and sustainability.

If left unmanaged, intramural competition can convert an ISA from a plus-sum game to a zero-sum game,[25] can produce a minus-sum downward spiral that results in the failure of the ISA, and in some cases can result in serious damage to one or both of the ISA partner companies.

Endnotes

1. The term *operational significance* is discussed in Chapter 1, Section 1.2.
2. This number is less than the total number of nation-states, because nation-states that are members of a currency union share the same currency. Currency unions are discussed in Section 10.1.1.2.
3. The euro is also used officially by four countries that are not EMU member states, and unofficially by two others.
4. In this context, the reserve currency countries are the US, the member countries of the European Monetary Union and other countries that use the euro, the UK, and Japan.
5. The exception to this principle is discussed in the last paragraph of this section.
6. The conflict of laws is discussed in Chapter 9, Section 9.1.2.
7. There are some exceptions to these requirements. For example, the US Supreme Court has ruled that, when operating in foreign countries, US companies are not required to comply with US laws relating to age discrimination and to some other human resources–related areas.
8. These instruments and mechanisms are discussed in Chapter 9, Section 9.1.4.
9. The term *global* is discussed in Chapter 6, Section 6.2.2.3.
10. The conflict of laws is discussed in Chapter 9, Section 9.1.2.
11. International transfer pricing is discussed in Section 10.1.1.4.
12. Political risk is discussed in Chapter 5, Section 5.5.
13. The surrogate third-country rule is discussed in Chapter 3, Section 3.1.5.

14. Subsidies are discussed in Chapter 3, Section 3.2; in Chapter 7, Sections 7.6.3.1 and 7.6.3.2; and in Chapter 9, Section 9.2.2.1.
15. Hofstede, *Culture's Consequences.*
16. The term *dichotomy* refers to a division between two things that are opposites or alternatives, or to a division from within a generic category or classification.
17. Hofstede, *Culture's Consequences,* 158.
18. The individualist–collectivist dichotomy is discussed in Section 10.2.2.3.
19. Hall, *Beyond Culture.*
20. The term *plus-sum* is discussed in Chapter 7, Endnote 4.
21. Davies, *Strategic Management,* 215–226 and Davies, Li, and Madan, "The TQM–Six Sigma Continuum."
22. Hofstede, *Masculinity and Femininity.*
23. Strategic alliances and ISAs are discussed in Chapter 4, Sections 4.1.1.1 and 4.3.3; and in Section 10.2.2.5.
24. Davies, *Partner Risk.* The term *partner risk* refers to the exposure by a partner in a strategic alliance to the possibility of opportunistic behavior by the other partner.
25. Game theory alternatives are discussed in Chapter 7, Endnote 4.

Abbreviations

ACTA: Anti-Counterfeit Trade Agreement
ADD: anti-dumping duties
AGOA: Africa Growth and Opportunity Act
AHM: American Honda Motor Co., Inc.
APHIS: Animal and Plant Health Inspection Service of the USDA
ASEAN: Association of Southeast Asian Nations
ASEAN FTA: Association of Southeast Asian Nations Free Trade Area
AU: African Union
BDV: Convention on the Valuation of Goods for Customs Purposes
CACM: Central American Common Market
CAN: Andean Community
CARICOM: Caribbean Community and Common Market
CBP: United States Customs and Border Protection
CCC: China Compulsory Certification
CCC: Customs Co-operation Council
CD: cultural difference
CETA: Canada–EU Comprehensive Economic and Trade Agreement
CFA: Central African Franc
CFIUS: Committee on Foreign Investment in the United States
CFP: Pacific Financial Community
CIS: Commonwealth of Independent States
CNCA: Certification and Accreditation Administration of China
CRO: WTO Committee on Rules of Origin
CSXWT: CSX World Terminals
CU: customs union
CUSFTA: Canada–US Free Trade Agreement
CVD: countervailing duty or anti-subsidy duty
DDTC: Directorate of Defense Trade Controls
DPI: Dubai Ports International
DPW: Dubai Ports World
DSB: Dispute Settlement Body of the WTO
DSM: dispute settlement mechanism
EAC: East Africa Community
ECOWAS: Economic Community of West African States

EEC: European Economic Community
EJV: equity joint ventures
EU: European Union
FDI: foreign direct investment
FPI: foreign portfolio investment
FSIS: Food Safety and Inspection Service of the USDA
FTA: free trade agreement, free trade area
GATS: General Agreement on Trade in Services
GATT: General Agreement on Tariffs and Trade
GCC: Gulf Cooperation Council
GSP: Generalized System of Preferences
HCCH: Hague Conference on Private International Law
HR: human resources
HS: Harmonized System
HTSUS: Harmonized Tariff Schedule of the United States
HTSUSA: Harmonized Tariff Schedule of the United States Annotated
IB: international business
IBRD: International Bank for Reconstruction and Development (World Bank)
ICC: International Chamber of Commerce
ICITO: Interim Commission for the International Trade Organization
ICJ: International Court of Justice (World Court)
ICSID: International Center for the Settlement of Investment Disputes
IMF: International Monetary Fund
IPR: intellectual property rights
IR: international relations
ISA: international strategic alliance
ISDS: Investor-State Dispute Settlement
ITI: Customs Convention on the International Transit of Goods
ITO: international trade organization
LAIA: Latin American Integration Association
MA: Marrakesh Agreement, Agreement Establishing the WTO
MERCOSUR: Southern Cone Common Market
MFN: most-favored nation
MOU: memoranda of understanding
MOUDC: Memorandum of Understanding on Drug Control
NAFTA: North American Free Trade Agreement
NATO: North Atlantic Treaty Organization
NTB: non-tariff barrier
OECD: Organisation for Economic Co-operation and Development
P&O: Peninsular and Oriental Steam Navigation Company
PE: post-entry barriers
PPA: Protocol of Provisional Application of the General Agreement on Tariffs and
　　　Trade
PTA: preferential trade area
RIA: regional integration agreement, regional integration area
ROO: rules of origin

RTA: regional trade agreement
RTB: regional trade bloc, regional trading bloc
SAARC: South Asian Association for Regional Cooperation
SACU: Southern African Customs Union
SADC: Southern African Development Community
SCM: Agreement on Subsidies and Countervailing Measures
SCO: Shanghai Cooperation Organization
SCT: separate customs territory
SOE: state-owned enterprise
TPA: trade promotion agreement
TRIMs: Agreement on Trade-Related Investment Measures
TRIPS: Agreement on Trade-related Aspects of Intellectual Property Rights
TRQ: tariff-rate quota
TSUS: Tariff Schedules of the United States
UAE: United Arab Emirates
UK: United Kingdom
UN: United Nations
UNCITRAL: United Nations Commission on International Trade and Law
UNCLOS: United Nations Convention on the Law of the Sea
UNCTAD: United Nations Conference on Trade and Development
UNESC: United Nations Economic and Social Committee
UNIDROIT: International Institute for the Unification of Private Law
US: United States
USDA: United States Department of Agriculture
USITC: United States International Trade Commission
USML: United States Munitions List
USTR: United States Trade Representative
WAEMU: West African Economic and Monetary Union
WCO: World Customs Organization
WIPO: World Intellectual Property Organization
WTO: World Trade Organization
WWII: Second World War

Bibliography

B1 Governmental and intergovernmental sources

B1.1 World Trade Organization sources

Agreement Establishing the World Trade Organization, Apr. 15, 1994. (Marrakesh Agreement) http://www.wto.org/english/docs_e/legal_e/04-wto_e.htm

Agreement on Rules of Origin, Apr. 15, 1994. http://www.wto.org/english/docs_e/legal_e/22-roo_e.htm

Agreement on Safeguards, Apr. 15, 1994. http://www.wto.org/english/docs_e/legal_e/25-safeg_e.htm

Agreement on Subsidies and Countervailing Measures, Apr. 15, 1994. (SCM) http://www.wto.org/english/docs_e/legal_e/24-scm_01_e.htm

Agreement on Technical Barriers to Trade, Apr. 15, 1994. http://www.wto.org/english/docs_e/legal_e/17-tbt_e.htm

Agreement on Trade-Related Aspects of Intellectual Property Rights, Apr. 15, 1994. (TRIPS) http://www.wto.org/english/docs_e/legal_e/18-trims_e.htm

Agreement on Trade-Related Investment Measures, Apr. 15, 1994. (TRIMs) http://www.wto.org/english/docs_e/legal_e/18-trims_e.htm

Appellate Body Report, *European Communities and Certain Member States—Measures Affecting Trade in Large Civil Aircraft*, WT/DS316/AB/R (May 18, 2011). http://www.wto.org/english/tratop_e/dispu_e/316abr_e.pdf

Appellate Body Report, *U.S.—Measures Affecting Trade in Large Civil Aircraft (Second Complaint)*, WT/DS353/AB/R (Mar. 12, 2012). http://www.wto.org/english/news_e/news12_e/353abr_e.htm

General Agreement on Tariffs and Trade, Oct. 30, 1947. (GATT 1947) http://www.wto.org/english/docs_e/legal_e/gatt47_01_e.htm

General Agreement on Tariffs and Trade, Apr. 15, 1994. (GATT 1994) http://www.wto.org/english/docs_e/legal_e/06-gatt_e.htm

General Agreement on Trade in Services, Apr. 15, 1994. (GATS) http://www.wto.org/english/docs_e/legal_e/26-gats_01_e.htm

Press Release, WTO Secretariat, *Azevêdo: Accessions work is a WTO priority*, Accessions, WTO: News Items, 2014, (Dec. 10, 2014). http://www.wto.org/english/news_e/news14_e/acc_10dec14_e.htm

———, *Days 3, 4 and 5: Round-the-clock consultations produce "Bali Package,"* WTO: News Items, 2013, (Dec. 7, 2013). http://wto.org/english/news_e/news13_e/mc9sum_07dec13_e.htm

————, *Lamy hails Russia's WTO accession ratification*, WTO: Press Releases, 2012, PRESS/668, (Jul. 23, 2012). http://www.wto.org/english/news_e/pres12_e/pr668_e.htm

————, *Let's make sure 2015 will be a year to remember for the WTO—Azevêdo*, General Council, WTO: News Items, 2014, (Dec. 11, 2014). http://www.wto.org/english/news_e/news14_e/gc_rpt_10dec14_e.htm

————, *Russia files dispute against the European Union over anti-dumping measures*, WTO: News Items, 2014, (Jan. 6, 2014). http://www.wto.org/english/news_e/news14_e/ds474rfc_06jan14_e.htm

————, *Ukraine—Definitive Safeguard Measures on Certain Passenger Cars*, Dispute DS468, WTO: News Items, 2014, (Oct. 8, 2014). http://www.wto.org/english/tratop_e/dispu_e/cases_e/ds468_e.htm

Protocol of Provisional Application of the General Agreement on Tariffs and Trade, Oct. 30, 1947. (PPA) http://www.wto.org/english/res_e/booksp_e/gatt_ai_e/prov_appl_gen_agree_e.pdf

Understanding on Rules and Procedures Governing the Settlement of Disputes, Apr. 15, 1994. (1994 Understanding) http://www.wto.org/english/docs_e/legal_e/28-dsu_e.htm

Understanding on the Balance-of-Payments Provisions of the General Agreement on Tariffs and Trade, Apr. 15, 1994. http://www.wto.org/english/docs_e/legal_e/09-bops.pdf

World Trade Organization, Ministerial Declaration of November 14, 2001. WT/MIN(01)/DEC/1 (Nov. 20, 2001) (Doha Declaration) http://www.wto.org/english/thewto_e/minist_e/min01_e/mindecl_e.htm#trips

WTO Secretariat, *Trade and Foreign Direct Investment*, New Report by the WTO, (Oct. 9, 1996). http://www.wto.org/english/news_e/pres96_e/pr057_e.htm

————, Trade topics, Market access for goods. http://www.wto.org/english/tratop_e/markacc_e/markacc_e.htm

————, *World Trade Report 2006: Exploring the links between subsidies, trade and the WTO*, (Jul. 7, 2005) http://www.wto.org/english/res_e/booksp_e/anrep_e/world_trade_report06_e.pdf

Note: WTO instruments can also be retrieved from http://www.wto.org/english/docs_e/legal_e/legal_e.htm

B1.2 United Nations sources

Charter of the United Nations (UN Charter), Jun. 26, 1945. http://www.un.org/en/documents/charter/

Permanent Sovereignty over Natural Resources, G.A. res. 1803, 1962. http://www.un.org/ga/search/view_doc.asp?symbol=A/RES/1803%28XVII%29

UN Commission on International Trade Law (UNCITRAL), *Convention on the Recognition and Enforcement of Foreign Arbitral Awards*, 1958. http://www.uncitral.org/uncitral/en/uncitral_texts/arbitration/NYConvention.html

————, *UN Convention on Contracts for the International Sale of Goods*, 1980. http://www.uncitral.org/uncitral/uncitral_texts/sale_goods/1980CISG.html

UN Conference on Restrictive Business Practices, United Nations Conference on Trade and Development (UNCTAD), *United Nations Set of Principles and Rules on Competition*, 1980, last updated 2010. http://www.unctad.info/en/6th-UN-Conference-on-Competition-Policy/

UN List of Least Developed Countries. http://www.unohrlls.org/en/ldc/25/

UN Office of Legal Affairs, Treaty Section, United Nations Treaty Handbook. http://treaties.
un.org/Pages/Publications.aspx?pathpub=Publication/TH/Page1_en.xml
———, Treaty Reference Guide, updated Jun. 1, 2014. http://treaties.un.org/Pages/Overview.
aspx?path=overview/definition/page1_en.xml
UN Secretariat, The UN System: Structure and Organization. http://www.un.org/en/aboutun/
structure/index.shtml
Vienna Convention on the Law of Treaties (1969). http://UN.untreaty.un.org/ilc/texts/
instruments/.../conventions/1_1_1969.pdf

B1.3 *United States sources*

Office of the United States Trade Representative, Investor-State Dispute Settlement (ISDS).
https://ustr.gov/about-us/policy-offices/press-office/fact-sheets/2015/march/investor-
state-dispute-settlement-isds
Press Release, US International Trade Commission, *Frozen Warmwater Shrimp from
China, Ecuador, India, Malaysia, and Vietnam Do Not Injure U.S. Industry, Says
USITC*, News Release 13-091, Sep. 20, 2013. http://www.usitc.gov/press_room/news_
release/2013/er0920ll1.htm
US Customs and Border Protection, *What Every Member of the Trade Community Should
Know About: NAFTA for Textiles and Textile Articles*, Informed Compliance Series,
May 2008. http://www.cbp.gov/linkhandler/cgov/trade/legal/informed_compliance_
pubs/icp003r2.ctt/icp003.pdf
———, *What Every Member of the Trade Community Should Know about U.S. Rules of
Origin*, Informed Compliance Series, May 2004. http://www.cbp.gov/linkhandler/
cgov/trade/legal/informed_compliance_pubs/icp026.ctt/icp026.pdf
US Department of Agriculture, Animal and Plant Health Inspection Service. http://www.
aphis.usda.gov/wps/portal/aphis/ourfocus/importexport
———, FSIS Office of International Affairs. http://www.fsis.usda.gov/wps/wcm/
connect/7c1f9c3a-f063-4bef-80d0-895038a1af88/OIA_Brochure.pdf?MOD=AJPERES
US Department of the Treasury, *G:ITICFIUS Case 05-60 Dubai-P&OE-F Fact Sheet wit*,
Feb. 24, 2006. http://www.treasury.gov/press-center/press-releases/Pages/js4071.aspx
US Food and Drug Administration, *FDA 2013 Annual Report on Food Facilities, Food
Imports, and FDA Foreign Offices*, 2013. http://www.fda.gov/Food/GuidanceRegulation/
FSMA/ucm376478.htm
US Government Accountability Office, *U.S. Customs Service: Prospective Rulings More
Timely, but Database Reliability Questions Remain*, GAO-03-828, Aug. 2003. http://
www.gao.gov/products/GAO-03-828
US International Trade Commission (USITC), *Harmonized Tariff Schedule of the United
States (2015)*, (HTSUS). http://hts.usitc.gov
———, *Harmonized Tariff Schedule of the United States, by Chapter*, Jun. 30, 2014. http://
www.usitc.gov/tata/hts/bychapter/index.htm
US State Department, Directorate of Defense Trade Controls (DDTC), Mission. http://
pmddtc.state.gov
———, DDTC, Country Policies and Embargos. http://pmddtc.state.gov/embargoed_
countries/index.html
US Supreme Court, Worcester v. Georgia, 31 US (6 Pet.) 515, 561 (1832). http://supreme.justia.
com/cases/federal/us/31/515/case.html

B1.4 Other governmental and intergovernmental sources

ASEAN Declaration, Aug. 8, 1967. http://cil.nus.edu.sg/rp/pdf/1967%20ASEAN%20 Declaration-pdf.pdf

ASEAN FTA Secretariat. http://www.asean.org/asean/asean-secretariat

ASEAN Trade in Goods Agreement: Annex 8, *Operational Certification Procedures for the Rules of Origin of the ASEAN Common Effective Preferential Tariff Scheme for ASEAN Free Trade Area*, 1992, revised 2009. http://www.asean.org/communities/ asean-economic-community/item/operational-certification-procedures-for-the-rules- of-origin-of-the-asean-common-effective-preferential-tariff-scheme-for-asean-free- trade-area

Charter of the Association of Southeast Asian Nations (ASEAN), 2008. http://www.asean. org/asean/asean-charter/asean-charter

Charter of the Cooperation Council for the Arab States of the Gulf (GCC), 21 Rajab 1401, corresponding to May 25, 1981. http://www.gcc-sg.org/eng/indexfc7a.html?action=Sec- Show&ID=1

Convention on the Settlement of Investment Disputes Between States and Nationals of Other States, 1965, amended 2006. (ICSID Convention) https://icsid.worldbank.org/ICSID/ ICSID/RulesMain.jsp

Cooperation Council for the Arab States of the Gulf (GCC), Areas of Cooperation Achievements. http://www.gccsg.org/eng/indexa3c2.html?action=SecShow&ID=47

European Commission, EU Transparency Portal. http://ec.europa.eu/transparency/index_ en.htm

GCC Secretariat. http://www.gcc-sg.org/eng/index13ac.html?action=Sec-Show&ID=36

———, Foundations and Objectives. http://www.gcc-sg.org/eng/index895b.html?action=Sec- Show&ID=3

———, Implementation Procedures for the GCC Customs Union. http://www.gcc-sg.org/eng/ index9038.html?action=Sec-Show&ID=93

———, The Most Important Political and Strategic Objectives. http://www.gcc-sg.org/eng/ index15af.html?action=Sec-Show&ID=48

Hague Conference on Private International Law (HCCH), Convention on the Service Abroad of Judicial and Extrajudicial Documents in Civil or Commercial Matters, 1965. http:// www.hcch.net/index_en.php?act=conventions.text&cid=17

HCCH Convention on the Taking of Evidence Abroad in Civil or Commercial Matters, 1970. http://www.hcch.net/index_en.php?act=conventions.text&cid=82

International Center for the Settlement of Investment Disputes (ICSID) Secretariat. https:// icsid.worldbank.org/ICSID/Index.jsp

International Court of Justice, Statute of the International Court of Justice, 1945, revised 2007. http://www.icj-cij.org/documents/index.php?p1=4&p2=2&p3=0&

International Institute for the Unification of Private Law (UNIDROIT), Convention on International Interests in Mobile Equipment, 2001, last updated 2013. http://www. unidroit.org/instruments/security-interests/cape-town-convention

———, Convention on Stolen or Illegally Exported Cultural Objects, 1995. http://www. unidroit.org/instruments/cultural-property/1995-convention

North American Free Trade Agreement, 1992 (entered into force 1994). https://www.nafta- sec-alena.org/Home/About-the-NAFTA-Secretariat

North American Free Trade Agreement (NAFTA) Secretariat. https://www.nafta-sec-alena. org/Home/About-the-NAFTA-Secretariat

Organisation for Economic Co-operation and Development, *OECD Benchmark Definition of FDI, 4th edition*, 2008. http://www.oecd.org/daf/inv/investmentstatisticsandanalysis/fdibenchmarkdefinition.htm

Shanghai Cooperation Organization (SCO) Secretariat. http://www.sectsco.org/

Treaty of Amity and Commerce Between the United States and France, 1778. http://avalon.law.yale.edu/18th_century/fr1788-1.asp

World Customs Organization (WCO), Convention Establishing a Customs Co-operation Council, 1950. http://www.fd.uc.pt/CI/CEE/OI/WCO/convention_establishing_a_custom_cooperation_council.htm

———, International Convention on the Harmonized Commodity Description and Coding System (HS Convention), 1983 (entered into force 1988). http://www.wcoomd.org/en/about-us/legal-instruments/~/link.aspx?_id=002DC5117CE94EE1BC4B6BFFF4319BE9&_z=z

———, International Convention on the Simplification and Harmonization of Customs Procedures, 1974. (Kyoto Convention) http://www.wcoomd.org/en/about-us/legal-instruments/conventions.aspx

World Intellectual Property Organization, Convention Establishing the World Intellectual Property Organization, 1967, amended 1979. http://www.wipo.int/treaties/en/convention/trtdocs_wo029.html

B2 Articles and books

Agama, Laurie-Ann, and Christine A. McDaniel. "The NAFTA Preference and US-Mexico Trade, Office of Economics Working Paper." *US International Trade Commission* (October 2002). http://www.usitc.gov/publications/332/working_papers/ec200210a.pdf

Associated Press. "Malaysia Relaxes Foreign Investment Rules." *Jakarta Post* (June 30, 2009). http://www.thejakartapost.com/news/2009/06/30/malaysia-relaxes-foreign-investment-rules.html

Baldwin, Robert. "Anti-Dumping Ruling to Benefit Local Currant Industry." *Ministers for the Department of Industry* (14 January, 2014). http://minister.innovation.gov.au/ministers/baldwin/media-releases/anti-dumping-ruling-benefit-local-currant-industry

Davies, Warnock. "Beyond the Earthquake Allegory: Managing Political Risk Vulnerability." *Business Horizons* (July/August 1981): 39–43.

———. "Global Business Strategy: The Trade–Foreign Investment Dichotomy." *Journal of Transnational Management Development* 5, no. 1 (2000): 81–87.

———. *Partner Risk: Managing the Downside of Strategic Alliances* (West Lafayette, IN: Purdue University Press, 2000).

———. *Strategic Management,* 2nd ed. (Beijing: Science Press, 2011).

———. "The Choice of Quality Management Methods: The TQM–Six Sigma Continuum and its Application in China and India." *Business Vision*, 5 (1), January–June 2009. Co-authors: Li Shengxiao and Pankaj Madan.

———. "Unsticking the State of the Art of Political Risk Management." *Sloan Management Review* (Summer 1981): 59–63.

De Vera, Ben Arnold O. "US to Pursue Anti Dumping Case vs. Philippines 8 Others Over Oil Industry Pipe Imports." *InterAksyon.com* (August 19, 2013). http://www.interaksyon.com/business/68880/us-to-pursue-anti-dumping-case-vs—philippines-8-others-

Ghafour, P. K. Abdul. "KSA [Kingdom of Saudi Arabia] wins anti-dumping case against India." *Arab News, Jeddah* (November 18, 2013). http://www.arabnews.com/news/479306

Giannoulis, Karafillis. "EU Imposes Biodiesel Anti-Dumping Duties." *NewEurope Online* (November 21, 2013). http://www.neurope.eu/article/eu-imposes-biodiesel-anti-dumping-duties

Hall, Edward T. *Beyond Culture* (Garden City, NY: Anchor Press/Doubleday, 1976).

Hernandez, Alejandra M. "Venezuela's Chávez orders expropriation of Owens Illinois local unit." *El Universal* (October 26, 2010). http://www.eluniversal.com/2010/10/26/en_eco_esp_venezuelas-chavez-o_26A4654891

Hofstede, Geert. *Culture's Consequences, International Differences in Work-Related Values* (Beverly Hills: Sage Publications, 1980). http://geert-hofstede.com/publications.html

———. *Masculinity and Femininity: The Taboo Dimension of National Cultures (Cross Cultural Psychology)* (Beverly Hills: SAGE Publications, 1998).

Hudec, Robert E. "The Role of the GATT Secretariat in the Evolution of the WTO Dispute Settlement Procedure." In *The Uruguay Round and Beyond: Essays in Honour of Arthur Dunkel*, edited by Jagdish Bhagwati and Mathias Hirsch, 101–120. Ann Arbor: University of Michigan Press, 1998.

Index

About the author

Warnock Davies has spent most of his career in strategy and international business in the private sector and in academia.

In the private sector, he has worked as a consultant and task force leader with major multinational corporations and mid-sized companies on the formulation and implementation of corporate, business-unit, and project-specific international business strategies—and has provided advice and assistance on the structure and management of foreign direct investment operations in 40 countries. His executive appointments have included vice president at Business International Corporation and president and CEO of a publicly listed company.

In academia, he has held professor or visiting-professor appointments at Mercer University, the University of Colorado, Nanyang Technological University, Lahore University of Management Sciences, and Shaoxing University; has taught strategy and international business in MBA and executive programs at these and other universities; and has served as dean of the School of Management at Golden Gate University.

He currently consults to private sector clients on strategy and international business—and designs and delivers corporate seminars in these same areas.

He holds a PhD in international business and international relations, an MALD in civilization and foreign affairs, and an MA in international law from the Fletcher School of Law and Diplomacy at Tufts and Harvard Universities.

He can be contacted at warnock-davies@outlook.com